EARNING THE RIGHT TO

BE HEARD

EARNING THE RIGHT TO

BE

HEARD

SELL YOUR **IDEAS**
BUILD YOUR **INFLUENCE**
GROW YOUR **OPPORTUNITIES**

PHILLIP VAN HOOSER

Published and distributed by:
SOUND WISDOM
P.O. Box 310
Shippensburg, PA 17257-0310
717-530-2122

info@soundwisdom.com

www.soundwisdom.com

While efforts have been made to verify information contained in this publication, neither the author nor the publisher assumes any responsibility for errors, inaccuracies, or omissions. While this publication is chock-full of useful, practical information; it is not intended to be legal or accounting advice. All readers are advised to seek competent lawyers and accountants to follow laws and regulations that may apply to specific situations. The reader of this publication assumes responsibility for the use of the information. The author and publisher assume no responsibility or liability whatsoever on the behalf of the reader of this publication.

ISBN 13 TP: 978-1-64095-324-6

ISBN 13 eBook: 978-1-64095-325-3

For Worldwide Distribution, Printed in the U.S.A.

1 2 3 4 5 6 7 8 / 25 24 23 22 21

DEDICATION

This book is dedicated to the memory of the late Jerry Brenda.

Jerry's unfailing encouragement informed, inspired, and directed my thinking, work, and career for more than 40 years.

I am better because of the ideas, influence, and opportunities Jerry provided me.

ACKNOWLEDGMENTS

Acknowledgments might seem relatively unimportant to most readers, but not to this author. This book would have remained uninspired, unwritten, unedited, unpublished, and undelivered had each of the following people not played a significant role in moving it forward.

I begin with Art Malek and the late Jerry Brenda. I've never met two finer examples of molders of young talent. Art was my first plant manager and Jerry my first manager. Both taught me many things at a young age, including the value of taking a good idea and helping others understand its possibilities.

My friend and fellow speaker/author Sam Silverstein generously introduced me to David Wildasin, publisher of Sound Wisdom. In turn, Dave expanded my Sound Wisdom network to include editor and director of content strategy, Dr. Jennifer Janechek; Eileen Rockwell, cover and graphic designer; and Christina Lynch, office manager. This book is a FAR better version of itself due directly to Jen's involvement. This book's cover design is representative of Eileen's trained eye and focused efforts. This book is in your hands due to Christina's administrative and logistical skills. Of course, David made it all possible by inviting me to be a part of the Sound Wisdom team. To all these wonderful folks, I'm grateful.

Throughout the writing process, my Van Hooser Associates, Inc., team had my back, freeing me up to do whatever needed to be done. Alyson Van Hooser, my daughter-in-law and business partner, is a fine speaker, writer, and businesswoman. Beyond that, her appreciation for the value of the *Earning the Right to Be Heard* process and possibilities is well known. I appreciate her consistently urging me to write this book for those whom it can help.

Finally, Susan Van Hooser, my wife and business partner for 36 years. Beautiful and intelligent, she's also skillful, savvy, strategic, organized, and exceptionally hardworking. We've done this all before and will probably do it again. But I can't imagine us doing it without one another.

So there you have it. Critically important people who have come together in order for you to have access to the lessons this book contains. It's our pleasure to provide these *Earning the Right to Be Heard* opportunities to you.

CONTENTS

Introduction 17

SECTION 1: UNDERSTANDING THE CONCEPT 19

Chapter 1   Sellers and Buyers. 21
            Questions to Begin 21
            Roles and Responsibilities. 23
            Expanding Your Influence 24
            The Question Continuum 27
            Establishing the Premise 28
            Selling Yourself First 31
            Sellers Are Great, Buyers Are Better 31
            A Concise Review 33

Chapter 2   Tangible Products vs. Intangible Ideas. 35

Teeing It Up 35

Tangible Products 36

Formal Processes Are Never Haphazard 37

Too Busy to Think 38

Intangible Ideas 40

One More Look 41

A Concise Review 42

Chapter 3   Two Fundamental Truths 43

The Way You Do What You Do 43

Two Practical Questions 46

Decision-Makers Are Key 48

Fundamental Truth #1: Passion and Emotion 49

Fundamental Truth #2: Logic and Rationale 50

If This, Then That 52

A Concise Review 53

Chapter 4   Two Foundational Objectives 55

Knowing Where You're Going 55

A Plan Takes Shape 59

First One, Then the Other 61

Foundational Objectives Prioritized 66

Losing the Right to Be Heard 67

Jack and Rick's Postscript 69

A Concise Review 71

SECTION 2:   SETTING THE STAGE 73

Chapter 5 **The Foundation of Influence** 75

Intentional Influence 75

The Five C's of Influence 76

A Concise Review 84

Chapter 6 **Starting Strong** 85

The Risk Reward 85

First Steps 86

A Concise Review 90

Chapter 7 **Opening Statements** 91

Time Is Money 91

They Know a Thing or Two 92

Creative Ownership 93

Self-Inflicted Wounds 95

No Small Talk 96

Start Strong 97

A Concise Review 100

Chapter 8 **Five Key Questions** 101

Questions Propel Learning 101

The Question Continuum 102

Patience Is a Virtue 103

Charting the Flow 105

Five Key Questions 110

Sequence Happens 111

A Concise Review 112

Chapter 9   **How Much Will It Cost?** 115

     A Critical Juncture 115

     How Much Will It Cost? 116

     Three Wrong Answers 118

     The Proof Is in the Preparation 122

     Taking Care of the Little Things 128

     Direct and Indirect Costs 129

     The "Cost" Proof 132

     Never Pad 133

     Stand Firm 133

     Batting .500 Is Not the Objective 136

     A Concise Review 137

Chapter 10   **What Are the Benefits?** 139

     How Much Is Too Much? 139

     The Most Important Question 142

     What Benefits Can Be Expected? 143

     The "Benefits" Proof 145

     The Plausibility Factor 147

     Legitimately Defensible 149

     In the Spirit of Full Disclosure 152

     A Concise Review 153

Chapter 11   **How Much Time Will It Take?** 155

     Simple as 1–2–3 155

     When Can You Start? 156

How Much Time Will It Take? 157

The "Time" Proof 159

Time Is Money 160

Unidentified Needs and Expectations 162

Always Pad 163

A Concise Review 166

Chapter 12 How Difficult Will It Be to Implement? 169

Plan, Communicate, Execute 169

The Biggest Challenge Yet 173

Too Much May Not Be Enough 174

It's Not My Job 175

How Difficult Will It Be to Implement? 177

The "Implementation" Proof 179

Overview/Project Highlights 183

Overview/Recommended Implementation Plan 183

Project Organization Chart 183

Project Communication Strategy 185

Hypersensitivity Is Nonsense 187

A Concise Review 190

Chapter 13 What Are the Possible Consequences? 193

Expect the Unexpected 193

Unintended Consequences 195

Opportunities, Complacency, Execution 196

The Parable of the Talents 199

Proof Free 200

What Are the Consequences of Not Taking Action?............201

The Three Don'ts...202

A Firm Commitment.......................................203

Benefits, Benefits, Benefits..............................207

A Concise Review 211

SECTION 4: REALIZING THE PAYOFF 213

Chapter 14 What Now, What Next? 215

Cliff Hangers or Happy Endings? 215

This Is the Beginning 220

"Bearing" the Burden.....................................221

Wins and Losses 222

"I Suck at Quitting" 224

A Concise Review 227

Chapter 15 Loose Ends 229

Transformation Begins Here 229

Charting Your Results 230

What about Brenda? 235

The Process in Practice 236

FAQs 238

Yesterday...243

A Concise Review 246

Conclusion 247

"It Doesn't Work!".......................................247

Trust Yourself 249

About the Author 251

INTRODUCTION

I'm so glad you've chosen to invest your time, energy, and resources into this book and its possibilities. Believe me, there are real possibilities that await in the pages to come. Opportunities to learn more about a proven process for identifying, qualifying, quantifying, and introducing your ideas to those who can approve and support them. That's a big deal.

I've invested more than 25 years into developing, applying, and fine-tuning the *Earning the Right to Be Heard* process. It has proven itself to be exceptionally beneficial to me personally time and time again.

Years ago, I began teaching the process to interested organizations and individuals via professional workshops. I have taught the *Earning the Right to Be Heard* process at least 100 times. The results are always the same.

Organizations thank me for sharing a simple, yet effective means of structuring idea and project communication. Individuals thank me for removing the mystique and introducing a practical methodology for selling their ideas to decision-makers.

Therefore, the ultimate goal of this book is to transform—to change the structure, character, and appearance of—the way you approach idea preparation and presentation for the better. From that transformation can be expected to come expanded personal influence and increased opportunities.

You can do this. We can do this. Let's do this together.

SECTION 1:

UNDERSTANDING THE CONCEPT

CHAPTER 1

SELLERS AND BUYERS

Questions to Begin

Have you ever believed in something passionately?

Was it something you were convinced would be of significant benefit to others?

Was it something needing the approval of a decision-maker to become reality?

If so, you know that accomplishing your objective requires much more than just smooth talking and masterful "sales" tactics. Persuasion is about earning the right to be heard—in the moment and in the future—and it requires planning and practice. Regardless of whether you are "selling" an idea, a product, or a service, from this point forward, I will refer to that "something" generally as an "idea" or "initiative," for all proposals have, at their heart, a concept. The person presenting that initiative or idea to a decision-maker becomes the "idea seller." The decision-maker, therefore, becomes the "buyer."

The heart of the conversation to follow is about convincing real-world, dyed-in-the-wool, bona fide professional decision-makers (buyers) to listen intently to you (the seller) and your idea. If successful in earning the decision-maker's attention, the next objective is to have your idea approved via your fine-tuned "pitch." As will be reiterated throughout this book, the stakes of this proposal extend beyond the final "yes" or "no" you receive from the decision-maker. In the balance is also the amount of influence you will yield and opportunities you will be given in the future.

Maybe you have experience in such undertakings. It's certainly possible that in the past, you've pitched ideas to bankers, business associates, or bosses. Whomever it was and whatever your intended purpose, that individual wielded ultimate power—the power to approve the idea/initiative, defer it, or cause it to come to an unceremonious halt.

So what were the results?

Did the experience play out in a positive, collegial manner? Did the decision-maker afford you the level of professional attention you desired? Did the decision-maker listen carefully to your idea? Did your "pitch" receive solid approval and full support? Did the experience leave you feeling as if you and your idea were appreciated, your influence expanding, and your opportunities growing?

Or did your experience transpire much differently?

In a failed attempt to gain decision-making support for an idea or initiative, did the meeting devolve into an unpleasant, discordant scene? Was the decision-maker inattentive, disconnected, possibly discourteous? Were you peppered with seemingly random questions for which you had no ready answer? Did your "sales presentation" end (fizzle, really) inconclusively, with no clear determination regarding "next steps"? Did you leave the meeting discouraged, frustrated, possibly disillusioned?

Whatever your past results, good or bad, you're doing what you should be doing right now. You're reading this book. In so doing, you're sure to discover a valuable process. A process designed specifically to take the guesswork out of idea presentation. A process designed to garner decision-making attention and invite action. A process designed to build your influence and grow your opportunities. A process referred to as *Earning the Right to Be Heard*.

Roles and Responsibilities

For any business transaction to be successfully and expeditiously completed, two foundational roles must coexist and function in reasonable harmony. Sellers (of products or ideas) must know, accept, and fulfill their unique responsibilities, while buyers must do the same.

The roles and responsibilities of each party in any transaction are admittedly unique and far too frequently oblivious to the other. Not understanding or accepting the role of the other—whether seller or buyer—can produce unnecessary challenges to the transactional process at hand. When this happens, interactions become more confused, convoluted, and occasionally contentious. As bad as that sounds, the damage and frustration don't stop there. Whatever frustrations and negative impressions might be created or experienced during the transaction may haunt both transaction participants indefinitely. Challenges experienced today tend to linger long in the minds of those who experienced and worked through them.

Conversely, the better each transactional participant (seller and buyer) understands the other's motives and objectives, the greater the chance for a successful and mutually satisfying outcome. In other words, the best sellers and buyers among us don't focus solely on what they are selling or buying. The very best invest at least as much time, energy, and effort into understanding whom they're selling to or buying from, as well as what that person wants, needs, and values most from the transaction.

Expanding Your Influence

Every idea seller likes answers—after all, the ultimate goal is a favorable decision—but questions are the key to professional growth and the expansion of one's influence. It's the questions we ask ourselves before we pitch our idea, the questions we ask others as we conduct initial research on our proposal, and the questions we field from decision-makers that strengthen our ability to "sell" an idea or initiative and improve our standing over time.

I've always been the inquisitive type. As a child, I was driven by curiosity to ask my parents, grandparents, and various family members frequent questions. While my impromptu inquiries served me well early in life, I quickly learned in the professional world that there was a crucial methodology for asking and answering questions in a way that yielded positive results.

As a human resources supervisor, I spent several years of my career wandering in and out of individual offices and meetings, break rooms and board rooms, conference rooms and cafeterias—wherever team members worked and congregated. It was my responsibility to walk and talk, to look and listen, and above all to pay attention to what was going on throughout the organization. In so doing, I made note of various activities, often wondering why certain activities weren't being managed differently—better.

Why don't decision-makers know or act on this? I often wondered to myself. So I asked.

In my professional position, I enjoyed generally unrestricted access to various levels of decision makers. Early on, not knowing any better, I was guilty of catching individual decision-makers off guard with some of my unexpected questions. My questions were never intended to be "gotcha" moments, designed to intentionally embarrass the one being questioned. Rather, they were always intended to help identify new ideas and initiatives that could help make things better.

By approaching (a.k.a. blindsiding) various busy decision-makers with unexpected questions, I discovered that their reactions became predictable. The decision-maker, having not anticipated the incoming barrage, would quickly regroup and ask a series of their own questions. Their initial questions led to other questions.

Initially, with absolutely no evidence to support my knee-jerk assumption, I chose to believe the decision-maker's retaliatory questions were nothing more than intentional diversions—smokescreens, if you will, intended to derail my purpose and redirect my path.

But I was wrong. My intention in asking the questions was honorable; thus, the decision-maker's reactive questions frustrated me. I admit that. Excessive emotion occasionally clouded my thinking. I admit that, too. Nevertheless, I was still wrong. I eventually came to realize that decision-makers' intentions were honorable, as well.

My experiences brought me face to face with an important, albeit harsh, reality. I learned that professional decision-makers approach decision-making differently than most of the rest of us. Theirs is not a random, haphazard activity. For decision-makers to make good, defensible decisions, they must have clear-cut answers to specific questions.

Over time, I came to realize that if I helped provide decision-makers with information to aid their decision-making cause, the conversations that followed were more pleasant, the results more predictable, and my input and influence more appreciated. It can work that way for you, too.

Many hours have since been invested in reflecting on those early "Q&A" experiences, their outcomes, and the value of the lessons embedded in them. Careful consideration has revealed a foundational, sequential process that can be thought of as follows:

QUESTIONS PROPEL LEARNING;

LEARNING FUELS ADVANCEMENT;

ADVANCEMENT BUILDS INFLUENCE;

INFLUENCE GROWS OPPORTUNITIES; AND

OPPORTUNITIES INCREASE QUESTIONS.

The Question Continuum

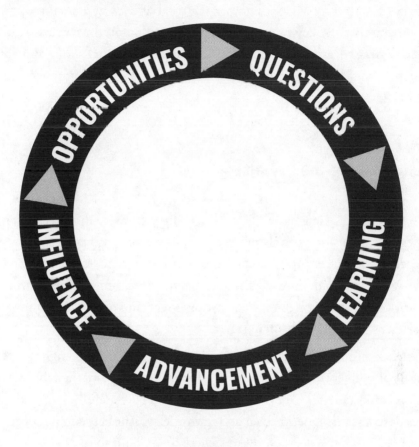

<u>Questions</u>

Sell Ideas
Build Influence
Grow Opportunities

This book will help you formulate and process questions in a way that builds your influence and increases your opportunities. As you read it, keep "The Question Continuum" (pictured above) in your mind, recognizing that the key to your short-term and long-term success is your willingness to anticipate questions and approach them as a valuable learning tool, rather than treating them like inconvenient or unnecessary obstacles.

Establishing the Premise

How others view our ability (or inability) to share information and ideas defines us—positively or negatively—in a very real and lasting way. In the workplace, professional decision-makers tend to remember us for what we do and how well we do it. Therefore, unnecessary communication breakdowns can have a lasting effect on your reputation, your relationships, and your influence.

Most professionals appreciate individuals who can get right to the heart of a subject quickly and directly. The more important the subject, the more important it is to deal with it directly and purposefully. If something needs to be said, done, or acted upon, why delay? The best communicators and most effective decision-makers know to get right to it.

This book falls into that category. Its subject is both important and challenging. It is a book written for those who genuinely desire to be high performers. It's a book that offers a practical perspective on what it really takes to build personal and professional influence with decision-makers at all levels.

Those who read and apply the strategies contained in the following pages are sure to discover a proven method for selling ideas and themselves more effectively. Included are practical tools, techniques, and processes necessary to continuously expand one's professional influence and impact.

Finally, once learned and applied, these practical lessons can be expected to yield previously unknown benefits and opportunities, which invariably reveal themselves through the act of *Earning the Right to Be Heard*.

It all begins by understanding and accepting the essential premise on which this book is based.

To better understand this foundational premise, consider four key words alongside their respective working definitions.

- SIGNIFICANT: important enough to be worthy of attention

- VALUE: the importance, worth, or usefulness of something

- SUCCESSFUL: achieving an aim or purpose

- SELLING: convincing someone of the merits of something

Individuals should expect personal recognition for the good work they do only if/when their contributions move some prized organizational initiative forward. Decision-makers are ultimately charged with making such "go/no go" determinations. If one can demonstrate to decision-makers that an idea or initiative is **SIGNIFICANT** because it is *"important enough to be worthy of attention,"* that idea or initiative can be expected to receive further consideration and scrutiny.

"Before significant value can be realized in our lives and work, successful 'selling' activities must take place."

It's important to remember, the **VALUE** of any initiative is ultimately determined by organizational decision-makers, NOT those individuals introducing or advocating for the initiative. Just because we claim something is important does not make it so. Having an initiative's *"importance, worth, or usefulness"* highlighted and acknowledged is a significant accomplishment—and a necessary step. But remember, the determination of value will always be in accordance with the organization's and decision-maker's standards of measurement, not necessarily your own. For this reason, it's critical to discover what those "value measurements" are in advance of any sales activity.

SUCCESSFUL identification of the merits associated with any significant initiative is critical. But wise influencers never overlook or ignore future challenges that might be experienced along the way as well. A fair and balanced presentation of both strengths and weaknesses works to clarify the initiative's actual value in *"achieving an aim or purpose."* Preemptive identification of possible concerns, weighed alongside trumpeted benefits, ultimately helps both the decision-maker and the person championing the initiative develop that required level of trust with one another.

Finally, in order to successfully accomplish the critical act of **SELLING** your initiative to decision-makers, the fine art of *"convincing someone of the merits of something"* is universally required. Getting a decision-maker to believe what you believe, then to embrace your suggestion, is far from being an easy task. But it's also not impossible. Highlighting (selling) an initiative's benefits, for example, is generally a far more convincing approach than attempting to sell on price alone.

Being able to skillfully combine these essential elements—*successfully selling significant value*—enhances one's chances of being acknowledged, being believed, and being influential.

Selling Yourself First

For a lot of people, the very idea of having to sell something is incredibly unpleasant. Even seasoned professionals have been known to expend tremendous amounts of energy disavowing themselves of almost all sales responsibilities. That's unfortunate, because in actuality we're all sellers, though most of us will rarely (if ever) be required to sell tangible products or services directly to others.

Nevertheless, we're still sellers, and the most significant, life-altering sales we make ultimately require the selling of ourselves. Never underestimate the importance of that sale. Selling yourself is a big deal. Business interactions, large or small, many or few, regularly revolve around how well or how poorly we sell ourselves first.

But it's important to note, selling yourself is not about talking a good game or playacting. Selling yourself requires (but is not limited to) the ability to sell successfully your personal values, strategic vision, emotional control, professionalism, and overall trustworthiness to others.

Yes, it's important for us to be continuously aware that we're always selling ourselves. Equally important is knowing who might be interested in buying what we're selling—and why.

Sellers Are Great, Buyers Are Better

Consider this oversimplified foundational statement: "for a seller to sell, a buyer must buy."

In this context of sellers and buyers, for the rest of your professional career you can reasonably expect to be a seller often, a buyer only occasionally. The reason is practical.

Regardless of your position, title, or seniority, your role as a seller emerges every time you wish to influence others with your ideas, initiatives, concepts, suggestions, or perspectives. As a seller, you attempt to effectively influence others to decide and act in a manner that ultimately favors your intent.

But remember, to be a successful seller, a decision-maker must buy. Despite the depth of your personal convictions, your preferred initiatives must first be bought by a decision-maker before they can be approved, supported, and acted upon. Rarely will you individually possess the authority (or resources) to make major buying decisions alone. Decision-makers/buyers not only make initial decisions—they usually are responsible for directing organizational resources as well.

Yes, the concept of this book is important and simple, but don't be fooled. It's never easy to master the task of selling yourself and your ideas. Think about it. If selling ideas to higher-level decision-makers was an easy task, virtually everyone would be secure in that process, right? But you and I know that most aren't secure. Insecurity causes too many otherwise capable professionals to gripe too much, worry too much, and in the end, accept far too little. Insecure individuals are quick to rationalize that things are the way they are because they've "always been that way and there's nothing I can do to change that." Those may be considered the final words of a defeated professional. I hope they are never heard from your lips.

This book was written to help otherwise capable, highly motivated team members who wish to make a discernible difference by way of their personal influence. When finished working through the pages that follow, you'll realize it's all here—a complete, step-by-step guide detailing a process not only for selling your ideas and initiatives more effectively to decision-makers, but also, and just as importantly, for selling yourself more consistently and confidently along the way.

A Concise Review

Questions propel learning; learning fuels advancement; advancement builds influence; influence grows opportunities; and opportunities increase questions.

"Before *significant value* can be realized in our lives and work, *successful 'selling'* activities must take place."

The *VALUE* of any initiative is ultimately determined by organizational decision-makers, NOT by those individuals introducing or advocating for the initiative.

Selling yourself requires (but is not limited to) the ability to successfully sell your personal values, strategic vision, emotional control, professionalism, and general trustworthiness.

Regardless of your position, title, or seniority, your role as a seller emerges every time you wish to influence others with your ideas, initiatives, concepts, suggestions, or perspectives.

CHAPTER 2

TANGIBLE PRODUCTS VS. INTANGIBLE IDEAS

Teeing It Up

In chapter 1, the overarching goal defining the process of *Earning the Right to Be Heard* was identified. Also introduced was a broad concept regarding "sellers" and "buyers" of ideas. In this chapter and those to follow, we'll further explore the seller/buyer dynamic, intentionally narrowing our focus with each succeeding chapter until the desired objective of *Earning the Right to Be Heard* has been fully accomplished.

Tangible Products

Here's a question to consider: Which is easier to sell—an intangible idea or a tangible product? It's a legitimate question with no clear-cut correct answer. Of course, some will argue the benefits or challenges of one over the other. After all, we all have preferences. Personal preferences are generally rooted in some unique combination of training, experiences, and personality types. But whether tangible or intangible, what should never be argued is the value of developing systematic processes for selling either—or both.

Like most people, my early professional training and experiences were foundational. My first post-college job introduced me to the previously unknown world of manufacturing. It was different than anything I had experienced at the time. I was enthralled. I marveled at the literally thousands of uniquely designed processes functioning all around me—each process designed to develop, build, and sell tangible products. The scope, magnitude, and sophistication of the processes I encountered extended well beyond my imagination. There were lessons to be learned at every turn.

One of the earliest of those lessons was that virtually nothing of significant value happened by chance. Every *tangible* ("perceptible by touch") *product* ("an article manufactured for sale") was the result of meticulous planning and conscientious follow-through. I learned the production processes around me were engineered to be logical, rational, and systematic. Each step of every process was somehow intended to support the further production, distribution, and sale of these tangible products.

I came to realize that every product represented months, sometimes years, of intricate planning and decision-making. Since the product was tangible, both the manufacturer/seller and buyer/user could reasonably evaluate its substance and quality at multiple points throughout the process.

Formal Processes Are Never Haphazard

There's another important thing I learned during my manufacturing years as a manager-to-be-in-training: formal processes support more than just tangible product creation; the intangible activities of planning and decision-making also require and benefit from systematic processes.

I came to realize that literally thousands of production processes went into the creation of every manufactured product. But each process was the tangible result of tens of thousands of independent, often intangible, decisions. These independent decisions themselves were made by countless anonymous decision-makers up and down the line.

It goes to reason that each of these anonymous decision-makers had themselves been methodically and systematically trained to make decisions in some predetermined manner. I know. That's what I was being trained to do. Once trained, each newly minted decision-maker was assigned organizational responsibility for ensuring various processes were followed so as to avoid, eliminate, or mitigate potential issues.

Of course, in the end, perfection is a conceptual myth. Not every decision is a good decision. We must remember that decisions are made by people, and people are fallible. It's also a fact that some decision-makers are simply more capable, more attentive, and more committed to their assigned duties and tasks than are others.

But the best, most consistently successful decisions always shared one sometimes not-so-obvious characteristic: they were anything but haphazard. Successful decisions were—and are—carefully made by conscientious decision-makers who are well-schooled and highly practiced in sound decision-making *processes*.

Please understand these last four paragraphs are not simple rhetoric and therefore are best not rushed through. In fact, I encourage you to reread them, this time searching for embedded *Earning the Right to Be Heard* "clues."

These clues provide a better understanding of why and how successful independent business owners and decision-makers make their best decisions. Clues as to why your best ideas, suggestions, and initiatives might have been rejected in the past. Most importantly, clues to prepare you to be better positioned to *Earn the Right to Be Heard* from those who will make decisions regarding your future ideas and initiatives.

Remember, the foundational objective of every independent decision-maker responsible for any significant organizational activity is to leave as little to chance as possible. Not only do professional decision-makers want to eliminate errors, but they also want to eliminate the future *possibility* of errors. The concept of "fixing something before it breaks" is rooted in sound decision-making logic and rationale, paramount to both building (and selling) tangible products and intangible ideas/initiatives.

In a practical sense, this is what solid decision-makers do: First, they strategize and plan. Second, they go about the process of managing those strategies and plans by utilizing a logical, rational, systematic mindset. This book is intended to teach you to do the same.

Too Busy to Think

In a very real sense, a lot of dedicated, exceptionally hardworking business professionals—sellers and buyers alike—sacrifice their precious ability to be more influential by allowing themselves to become too busy to think. For such individuals, the thought of spending time in deep, focused, uninterrupted thought and planning is tantamount to some sort of guilty, selfish pleasure. Many admit to being besieged with an overpowering urge to "do *something*." If caught "sitting, thinking, and planning," they fear others might adjudge them to be "stalling, loafing, and procrastinating."

But the opposite is true for the most successful and influential sellers and buyers. They have learned the value of careful, thoughtful preparation. For example, accomplished sellers of ideas intentionally pause long enough to carefully think through the idea or initiative they wish to promote. In doing so, they take the time necessary to consider the decision-maker's position and perspective. They intentionally explore the most creative ways to deliver their idea to the decision-maker for the greatest impact. They always have a process in place to follow—and they stick with it.

As for the decision-maker, he/she also benefits from time to think. When an idea seller approaches them, the most effective decision-makers don't blow them off or jump to conclusions "in the interest of time." They realize that they are generally well-served to pause, listen, then think carefully about the idea being offered. There are always questions to be asked. There are always answers to be considered. When sellers and buyers of ideas take the time to really engage with one another and the information being exchanged, good things have a way of happening.

In the end, the last thing either sellers or buyers of ideas should want to see happen is an idea being delivered, considered, or acted upon under duress due to inadequate time set aside or invested in its preparation or deliberation. Decisions made and actions taken under such circumstances are bound to be reactive and shortsighted. In these scenarios, it's obvious that little independent thought or strategic planning went into the decisions from either perspective. Both sellers and buyers who respond in such a way are more likely to lose influence with each other than to gain it.

Intangible Ideas

Let's revisit once more the degree of difficulty regarding selling tangible products versus intangible ideas. As stated earlier, one is not necessarily more difficult than the other. The degree of difficulty is determined by the requisite levels of training, experience, and of course, personal preference. For me, personally, I tend to believe it's harder to sell an intangible idea than a tangible product.

With a tangible product, you see what you have. You can lift it, move it, twist it, throw it, or even junk it if you wish. With the right process, minute-by-minute determinations can be made as to whether each new action undertaken has produced the desired result.

But an intangible idea is different. It's akin to a vapor. An intangible idea may represent a wisp of thought that can't be physically touched or captured. Even under ideal circumstances, intangible ideas can be exceptionally difficult to explain or understand, especially when first envisioned or introduced. That's one reason too many decision-makers initially reject and discard intangible ideas, though the idea might be presented by trusted, valued sellers.

For a seller to secure appropriate attention and consideration from a busy decision-maker, intangible ideas MUST be accompanied and supported by tangible, logical, rational criteria, plans, and processes. When one person doesn't have (or make) time to think about how something might work—another must!

Furthermore, these criteria and processes MUST align seamlessly with the decision-maker's own accepted decision-making processes and procedures. Otherwise, it's far too easy for even a well-meaning decision-maker to cast new intangible ideas aside with little thought or further consideration.

One More Look

WAIT! Don't miss that point!

Consider the critically important previous two paragraphs one more time before moving on. They read:

> **"For a seller to secure appropriate attention and consideration from a busy decision-maker, intangible ideas MUST be accompanied and supported by tangible, logical, rational criteria, plans, and processes. When one person doesn't have time to think about how something might work—another must!**
>
> **Furthermore, these criteria and processes MUST align seamlessly with the manager's own accepted decision-making processes and procedures. Otherwise, it's far too easy for even a good, well-meaning decision-maker to cast new, intangible ideas off without the immediate benefit of serious thought or further consideration."**

Here's the good news: Once you recognize and understand what a decision-maker wants and needs, the process becomes fairly easy. Once the right process is put into action, significant advances in individual influence can occur—and quickly. By presenting intangible ideas in ways that busy decision-makers are trained to think and prepared to act, significant strides—even breakthroughs—in the *Earning the Right to Be Heard* process can be made.

Of course, that's what I'm here for! To help you do just that.

A Concise Review

Processes for selling a tangible product versus an intangible idea are fundamentally different, and intangible ideas are arguably harder to sell to decision-makers.

The overarching objective of every overseer of any serious organizational activity is to leave as little to chance in his/her decision-making as possible.

Many skilled decision-makers are apt to reject and discard intangible ideas, even from trusted, valued team members, unless those ideas are accompanied and supported by tangible, logical, and rational criteria and processes.

Understanding what business professionals and decision-makers need and want in order to make effective decisions is a crucial first step in preparing any individual for *Earning the Right to Be Heard*—now and in the future.

CHAPTER 3

TWO FUNDAMENTAL TRUTHS

The Way You Do What You Do

Have you ever gotten in your own way? Have you ever attempted something important only to discover that you had unknowingly sabotaged your own efforts?

I have. More than once. However, more often than not I had no awareness that it was happening, why it was happening, or the damage I was inflicting upon myself as it happened—damage to my influence and my future opportunities. No one called me out. No one voluntarily addressed the issue with me. These lessons were tough, and tough lessons are often learned the hard way—by experience.

I've always been generally comfortable sharing my thoughts, ideas, and experiences with others, especially when invited to do so. In fact, I enjoy it. As a result, early in my career when superiors made sweeping statements like, "If you see something that can help make the organization better, please let someone know," I took them literally. My input had been invited. The least I could do was offer it—and I did. Regularly.

Unfortunately, often those conversations didn't go as I had expected or hoped. My comments were not always embraced in a welcoming, appreciative manner. Sadly, over time I grew to detest the nagging feeling that for some unstated reason, my ideas, perspectives, and opinions were not being heard. Or if heard, they seemed not to be taken seriously. For reasons unknown to me, my carefully considered ideas and suggestions appeared to be of little to no concern or value to those who had invited them and with whom rested the power to embrace and implement them.

Can you relate? If so, you can imagine how discouraging it all was. I think most of us believe our ideas and suggestions are worthy, important, and of value on some level. Otherwise, why would we waste precious time considering, developing, and presenting those ideas when invited to do so?

As my discouragement grew, I found it to be personally galling to have invested time developing some idea, only to see no reciprocal interest or response from decision-makers. Whenever that happened, my frustration grew accordingly. Right or wrong, I took it personally.

A lot of time has passed since those early days. Thankfully, I've learned a few things along the way. For example, I've learned that when certain people ask for an opinion, they really don't want to hear it, especially if that opinion happens to differ from their own. Occasions such as these are little more than public theater, a drama directed to those who might be watching and impressed by it. You can be sure the same happens to almost all of us now and then.

But there's an even more important—and valuable—thing that I've learned. Today when I'm asked for my opinion or input, I now know how to deliver that message or information in a way more apt for it to be received and welcomed. I've learned that what we say (the message) is important. But I've also learned that how we choose to say it (the method) is often more important.

Although embarrassing to admit today, I now realize how poorly I mishandled too many of my early attempts at selling ideas to decision-makers. In retrospect, I recognize that I not only made mistakes, but often the same mistakes repeatedly. I just kept doing what I knew to do, what I'd always done, hoping it would work. If/when I was lucky enough to get a positive, receptive response, great. However, if/when unsuccessful, I gave little consideration as to whether my unsuccessful approach should be tweaked, overhauled, or jettisoned completely.

It may be the same for you. Rarely do we voluntarily take the time to dissect our failed attempts to determine their root cause. Instead of ferreting out the problem, far more often we ignore it, or blame others for it, and in the end repeat it.

Instead of examining our attitudes and actions to see if either might have been at fault, many of us prefer to blame decision-makers, the process, or even bad timing as the primary cause(s) for our failures. For too many of us, it's much easier to believe "someone did me wrong" than to evaluate honestly "what I did wrong" in terms of preparation and performance.

But the good news is this: I eventually learned to do just that—to reevaluate what I was doing right or wrong. I consciously abandoned my "go-to" excuses in pursuit of new truths and tactics to support those truths. I questioned what I needed to know and do. Equally important, I questioned what I needed to know—and stop doing. Now I'm ready to share both.

Always remember, what you do is important. The way you do it may even be more so. That became much clearer once I learned two fundamental truths.

Two Practical Questions

There are two practical, straightforward questions I'd like you to take a moment right now to seriously consider.

Question #1: During your professional career, have you ever attempted to introduce (sell) an idea or proposed action to a decision-maker (or group of decision-makers) who occupied a position of authority greater than your own? If so, take a few minutes to revisit and recall that particular experience.

- What decision-makers were involved?

- How important was the idea/proposed action to you at the time?

- How prepared did you feel in introducing the idea/ proposed action?

- How did the decision-maker make you "feel" in the room that day?

- What was the attitude of the decision-maker as the meeting began?

- What (if any) memorable statements were made by the decision-maker?

- What emotions did you experience as you made your formal "pitch"?

Question #2: What was the end result of your efforts?

- Were you pleased with the quality and effectiveness of your presentation?

- Did you feel as if you and the decision-maker truly connected?

- Did you feel the decision-maker understood your reasoning for the request?

- Were any unexpected outcomes (surprises) experienced?

- What was the attitude of the decision-maker as the meeting ended?

- Were you satisfied with the experience and the overall results?

- Did your relationship with the decision-maker(s) change in any way afterward?

If successful in getting what you wanted, I'm betting the experience, as satisfying as it was, is harder to recall in detail than if you didn't get what you wanted. For most people, failure has a way of enhancing negative experiences and searing unpleasant feelings into our mental bank of readily accessible memories. Unfortunately, those same memories can become barriers that need to be overcome in anticipation of and preparation for similar situations that can be expected to follow.

Decision-Makers Are Key

The questions asked in the previous section are critically important. I hope you didn't rush past them or skip them altogether. How can you know where you're going (or wish to go) unless you're exceptionally clear regarding where you've been and what you've experienced getting there? More specifically, how can you know what needs to be repeated or reworked unless you're clear on the good, the bad, and the ugly of similar past experiences?

In considering my own history, I stumbled on a revelation. In consciously thinking less about myself and more about the situations, the surroundings, and most importantly, the decision-makers I've encountered along the way, I discovered that independent business owners and those responsible for organizational decision-making are remarkably similar, even predictable, in their approach to making important decisions. Professional decision-making isn't a haphazard occurrence. It never has been. Most key decision-makers in organizations today are trained (formally, experientially, or both) to follow a prescribed, formatted, proven methodology for making sound business decisions.

I won't expose that process just yet. I will. It's coming shortly. Expect five full chapters dedicated to accomplishing that task in the pages ahead. Instead, right now we'll consider the two fundamental truths from which this universal decision-making process evolves.

Fundamental Truth #1: Passion and Emotion

This first fundamental truth involves those selling ideas and not the decision-makers at all. The hard truth is this: most untrained, unprepared individuals attempt to "sell" ideas based on a volatile concoction of personal PASSION and raw EMOTION.

It's possible this simple pronouncement of truth may produce an "aha" moment for some reading this just now. An epiphany. But frankly, I hope not. Instead, I hope you read this section and think, "Well, I knew that!" But believe me, not everyone does.

You see, many individuals, especially those casually schooled in the art of personal selling and influence-building, often are strongly encouraged—even explicitly taught—that the act of selling anything (products, services, ideas) is better served with heaping sides of emotion and passion.

What other possible way might one move (motivate) a prospective buyer (decision-maker) toward the desired buying mindset if not by way of heightened passion and emotion? For advocates of this sales technique, the exertion of pressure via exaggerated promises (or implied threats) is not only appropriate, but encouraged—possibly required.

Vivid mental images of overly exuberant, often brusque salespeople attempting to emotionally browbeat you (or anyone) into making a particular decision are hard to dismiss, erase, or reconcile. Certainly, no one wishes to be the recipient of such unpleasant advances. However, too many of us fall back on such techniques simply because no other viable sales options appear available.

When considering the appropriateness or inappropriateness of exuberant passion and emotion in selling almost anything, the old saying

"If the only tool one has is a hammer, then every problem looks like a nail" comes to mind. If an untrained salesperson believes he/she must force, coerce, or otherwise "talk someone into" something in order to be successful, then passion and emotion become inevitable—the hammers. They appear to be the most readily available tools for the job at hand. For such poorly trained individuals, every sales situation begins to look like a nail that needs to be hammered again and again with all the passion and emotion they can muster.

We must be honest. Since passion and emotion are too often used to control, force, even coerce a decision, even the slightest dependence on passion and emotion in an effort to influence a decision-maker can become overblown and ultimately lead to our downfall. You will see soon enough how both passion and emotion can actually hinder, not help, an individual's efforts to *Earn the Right to Be Heard*.

Fundamental Truth #2: Logic and Rationale

My second and more important realization regarding how decision-makers think is represented in the second truth. Plainly stated, most trained decision-makers base their individual "buying" decisions on solid, foundational, defensible techniques involving LOGIC and RATIONALE.

The use of "logic and rationale" as a counterpoint to "passion and emotion" is simple. Trained decision-makers possess the power and authority to say "yes" or "no," "you can" or "you can't," "we will" or "we won't." These are straightforward decisions. They are not intended to elicit excessive emotion, because that's not how the decision-maker is thinking when he/she makes the decision.

In truth, decision-makers are trained NOT TO MAKE decisions in the heat of the moment, but rather on the basis of systematic logic and defensible rationale. In essence, before committing to any course of action, decision-makers are trained to ask and answer two questions:

1. Does this decision make good business sense?

2. Will I be able to defend the rationale on which this decision has been made?

Remember this: The rationale behind well-formed decisions is intentional. It's always meant to align decisions and actions with organizational goals, objectives, and prevailing expectations. Trained decision-makers understand the yardstick in use. The quality of their decisions will be weighed against organizational metrics such as strategic plans, budgets, timelines, competitive pressures, compliance standards, consumer ratings, employee morale, and the like.

Make no mistake, there is a lot riding on virtually every decision a professional decision-maker renders. Besides obviously aiding or hindering the business cause, a decision-maker's reputation hangs in the balance as well. They will be known and remembered as much for the quality of the decisions they make as any other identifiable factor.

Decision-makers are certainly allowed to have strong feelings regarding any proposal presented for their consideration. However, those decision-makers know that regardless of how they feel, they are not free to make their decision based solely on those feelings. Sooner or later, the quality of every decision must be defended—and to increasingly higher levels of decision-makers: customers, supervisors/managers, executives, boards of directors, owners, shareholders, and ultimately the court of public opinion. "It just felt like the right thing to do at the time" is hardly a defense any decision-maker would feel comfortable basing his/her reputation, career, and future on. The unmistakable truth is that decision-making logic and rationale is the only logical and rational defense.

If This, Then That

So, what's the practical implication associated with understanding and aligning these "two fundamental truths" with our future efforts to positively influence behavior while *Earning the Right to Be Heard*?

It's essentially this. We must first accept that organizational buyers (decision-makers) truly base their buying decisions on the criteria of logic and rationale. Therefore, idea sellers (the rest of us) must consciously abandon all future expectations of influencing future buying decisions via the sole use of passion and emotion. Instead, we should redirect pent-up passion and emotion into developing and presenting logic and rationale in every future sales presentation or professional position statement.

A personal determination must be made—even right now. If how decision-makers buy is dependent on logic and rationale, then from this point forward, you must properly and intentionally utilize logic and rationale to sell your ideas to those decision-makers.

Smart, savvy, well-informed idea sellers can and should channel their passion and emotion toward learning and utilizing techniques specifically designed to *Earn the Right to Be Heard* by decision-makers everywhere.

Decision-makers, in turn, will more readily, even eagerly, embrace and welcome the sales criteria being offered by sellers due to a logical, rational path they can easily follow and relate to. For decision-makers, under such circumstances, it's not only easier to decide and commit; it's easier to defend and support such decisions once the commitment has been made.

A Concise Review

Too many people avoid the dissection of personal failures, preferring instead to blame decision-makers, processes, or even timing for poor results.

Fundamental Truth #1: Most unprepared and untrained individuals attempt to "sell" their ideas on the basis of their personal passion and emotion. However, sole dependence on passion and emotion can undercut our ability to influence others.

Fundamental Truth #2: Most trained decision-makers strive to base their "buying" decisions on defensible logic and rationale. They do so because sooner or later, the quality and reasoning behind every decision must be defended.

The rationale behind well-formed decisions is always intended to align every decision and its resulting action with the corresponding strategic goals, objectives, and prevailing limitations established by, or currently being experienced in, the organization.

Savvy sellers of ideas can and should channel their passion and emotion toward learning and utilizing the logical and rational criteria decision-makers use to determine a future course of action.

CHAPTER 4

TWO FOUNDATIONAL OBJECTIVES

Knowing Where You're Going

Over time I've had many memorable one-on-one conversations with would-be students, prospective employees, and aspiring entrepreneurs. Each, in his or her own way, communicated a personal request for my help regarding some activity deemed important and desirable to them individually. Unfortunately, too often the conversations went all wrong.

WOULD-BE STUDENT: "Mr. Van Hooser, would you write a letter of referral for me? I'm hoping to be accepted into State University in the fall. I understand State University is your alma mater. I thought a letter from you would be helpful."

ME: "That's exciting. Yes, I'm a big fan of State University. Many of the opportunities I've enjoyed can be traced back to my studies there. What's your area of interest? What are your educational goals?"

WOULD-BE STUDENT: "Oh, I don't know. Nothing specific yet. I'll decide all that later. I figure I'll just enjoy my first two years of college life, then decide what comes next."

PROSPECTIVE EMPLOYEE: "Thank you, Mr. Van Hooser, for granting me this interview. I'm anxious to learn more about the open position you have here."

ME: "I appreciate your interest. Let's start by you telling me what you know about our company, what we do, and why you'd like to work here."

PROSPECTIVE EMPLOYEE: "Honestly, I don't know much at all. I live nearby and have seen the company sign when I've driven by. I recently heard there was an open position here. I need a job with insurance and benefits, so I thought I'd apply."

FLEDGLING ENTREPRENEUR: "Mr. Van Hooser, you don't know me, but I heard you speak recently. I'm calling to ask if you would consider mentoring me."

ME: (pause) "Well, I do work with select individuals on occasion. What specific areas are you looking for help with?"

FLEDGLING ENTREPRENEUR: "Now that's a good question. I really don't know. I was just hoping we could meet periodically and figure all that out as we go. I hope to have my own business someday. Since you've done that, I figured you might be a good place to start."

In case you're wondering, yes, I've actually had the conversations above. Multiple times. Multiple individuals. Really.

The dialogue here, not intended to be verbatim, represents a fair reenactment of far too many of those real-world conversations. Believe me, as their decision-maker of choice—the buyer of what each was selling—I was disappointed, put off even, by their pitches. Personal disappointment always makes it easier to disengage and back away from further involvement.

The reasons for my disappointment were simple and, I believe, universal. First, each initiated contact with me with no consideration of other activities I might have underway. Time is a terrible thing to waste. In the end, they ended up wasting both theirs and mine.

Second, though each was different, all three presented a personal request—something they alone wanted—without considering how it would impact anyone beyond themselves. It's fine to want something personally. But to disregard the wants, needs, and sacrifices of others in the singular pursuit of your own desires is seen as being selfish.

Finally, each individual was woefully unprepared to support his/her request with solid logic and rationale. Their respective requests were wrapped in a thin veneer of personal desire or passion and nothing else.

The would-be student seemingly had given little to no thought regarding long-term educational and career aspirations. Their singular stated goal? Party for a couple of years, then figure things out. It's extremely doubtful that the young person ever paused to consider how their performance in the classroom might affect them—and me—long term. If they did poorly those first two years, the university's black mark wouldn't just be on their record; it would go on mine as well. After all, I made the referral.

Cut him/her some slack, Phil, you may be thinking. *After all, s/he's just a kid. We all make mistakes when we're young.*

Okay then, let's turn our attention to the prospective employee. Grown men and women—the great majority of people reading this book—must all look for work on occasion. It's inevitable. But disrespecting the interview process by doing no preliminary research on the company, the position, or the person conducting the interview is a colossal waste of everyone's time—the interviewer's and the interviewee's. Let's face the facts: everyone needs a job, but employing the approach exhibited makes the chances slim to none that an offer will be forthcoming.

As for the aspiring entrepreneur... "Surely, Phil, you can appreciate someone with the grit and desire to start his or her own business endeavor?"

I certainly can, especially considering that I've traveled that long, bumpy road myself. Been there, done that, as they say. But I had a clear idea of where I was going and what it would take for me to get there. None of the three individuals depicted in these examples offered a shred of evidence to indicate they could say the same. In fact, unknowingly, they sent an exceptionally strong underlying counter-message:

- I want something for me;

- I'm not absolutely sure what it is that I want;

- But whatever it is, I need/want you to get it for me—or at least help me get it; and

- If/when I get it, I'm sure you'll see that it was worth your sacrifice and effort.

I'm sorry, but that just doesn't work for me. I'm pretty sure that it won't work for most diligent, professional decision-makers either. How could it? There's no apparent logical or rational underpinning for the buyer/decision-maker to cling to.

One more thing. The individuals in the examples above will eventually recognize the reality of NOT getting the referral, the job, and/or a new mentor. That's bad enough. But what's worse is that most will remain completely oblivious to their biggest loss—the loss of future influence. Make good impressions and future influence grows. Make poor impressions and not only is short-term gain forfeited, but the future opportunities that result from well-earned influence are squandered as well.

It's deeply unfortunate—sad even—to encounter people moving "full steam ahead" without any clear sense of where they're going.

A Plan Takes Shape

Yes, I've had a number of memorable conversations with individuals needing help that ended badly. The reasons why have been listed.

But I've had other conversations, too. Conversations that took a very different turn. They, too, were memorable, but for different reasons.

Many years ago, a friend invited me to lunch. I arrived to find my friends Jack and Rick already seated at a corner table, their backs to the wall. No surprise there. They were cops.

We three friends were about the same age—early 30s. Their careers were similar. Both had been sworn law enforcement officers for over a decade. Both were experienced in patrol, criminal investigations, and various "special duty" assignments. Most important, both were smart, well-trained, and dedicated.

There was one other similarity. Within recent months, both had been promoted from patrol officers to the rank of sergeant. Their promotions meant they now would be supervising patrol officers; as such, they became part of the department's "command staff."

I quickly learned the reason for the lunch invitation. They needed help.

A few weeks earlier, they attended one of their first departmental staff meetings. Present were all majors, captains, and lieutenants (the hierarchal chain of command), as well as other "lowly sergeants," as Rick and Jack liked to refer to themselves. The meeting was led by the chief of police. Toward the meeting's end, the chief issued a blanket challenge: "If anyone here can show me a way to introduce an effective community policing model to our city, I'll listen. The time is right, but I can't do it alone."

(NOTE: Don't get hung up on the concept of understanding "community policing." It's unnecessary. Simply think of this as a unique internal challenge such as those regularly faced by other organizations.)

The room fell silent. No hands were raised, nor words spoken. Soon the meeting was adjourned. My friends lunched together that day. Alone.

"Why?" I asked.

"No one wants to eat or talk with 'lowly sergeants' when 'higher ups' are available," they explained.

That day they discussed, then developed, a rough outline of a community policing plan. Both had recent patrol experience and believed in the concept of community policing. Both believed a functional plan could be constructed and therefore began formulating one on a napkin.

That had been a few weeks earlier, they explained. They had since met repeatedly to fine-tune their plan—a plan, they stressed, no one else in the department, including the chief, knew about. Now they were sharing it with me. Why?

"Phil, the components are all there," they told me. "We've done our homework. This plan can work. We just need to make sure the structure is right. And we need direction on how best to present it to the chief."

It was an exciting challenge, made more exciting by their level of excitement, anticipation, and preparation.

The plan seemed plausible to me. The city would be divided into two separate sections—east and west. Each section would have patrol officers assigned to that section exclusively. Such exclusivity should allow patrol officers the opportunity of getting to know the neighborhoods better and, more importantly, neighborhood businesses and residents.

The plan seemed solid. Nevertheless, I asked the guys four basic questions—questions that I also want you to ask yourself about the idea/initiative you are hoping to "sell" to a decision-maker.

First One, Then the Other

Consider each of the following questions carefully, then complete your responses.

Question #1:

What is the specific idea/initiative that you would like to see implemented?

_____

_____

_____

_____

Question #2:

Do you feel strongly enough about this idea/initiative to prepare a "pitch" for a key decision-maker? If so, do it. If no, why not?

_____

_____

_____

_____

Question #3:

Do you expect your efforts to elicit some sort of favorable action? Why?

_____

_____

_____

_____

Question #4:

Do you expect your efforts to elicit some sort of unfavorable action? Why?

_____

_____

_____

_____

Question #5:

If/when you develop and deliver your "pitch" to the key decision-maker(s), what will your ultimate objective be? What will a successful outcome look like?

_____

_____

_____

_____

Pause briefly for appropriate reflection on each of the questions above and your answers to them before reading further.

Question #1:

So what idea or initiative are you truly passionate and concerned about? Does it have to do with organizational productivity, profitability, safety, quality, expediency, team unity, customer service, employee engagement, personal advancement...what?

As it related to Jack and Rick's plan, the answer to this question was easy. Their idea/initiative was to present the chief with an effective community policing plan as requested. Their plan took into consideration the factors above but emphasized public safety, expediency, team unity, and customer (citizen) service.

Question #2a:

Is this idea or initiative important enough for you to put in extra effort to make something good happen? (Remember, if you're not willing to invest extra time and effort, probably nothing of substance will happen. If something of significance does happen *without* your time and effort, you have no legitimate personal claim to that success. It happened in spite of, not because of you.)

Jack and Rick's plan was important because it was a challenge they could get excited about, it could yield a positive result, and it could improve the department and the wider community. Finally, it was a plan they were uniquely qualified to develop and present due to their recent policing activities in their community's neighborhoods.

Question #2b:

If you are willing to make the extra effort but still doubt your efforts will elicit some sort of favorable action, is it because you've tried and been shot down before—or that you generally expect the worst in such situations?

Jack and Rick were new to their positions. Other than general nervousness about how to move forward, they did not hesitate based on previous experiences. They took the chief at his word and responded to his challenge.

Question #3:

What makes you think the decision-maker(s) might naturally lean in your direction if/when you make your pitch? Is it that what you will be pitching is so long overdue, so desperately needed, that it can no longer be overlooked or minimized? Is it because the timing is finally right? Is it because enough of the right people support the idea that a tipping point has been reached?

Jack and Rick clearly believed their plan could be embraced, approved, and implemented. In fact, they expected as much.

Question #4:

What makes you think the decision-maker(s) might oppose or reject your idea and presentation out of hand? Is there anything you can do to control or mitigate such opposition?

Jack and Rick were pragmatic. They accepted the fact that a potential downside existed. They knew some of the command staff might harbor resentment, wondering, *Why should the chief trust a plan conceived by two "lowly sergeants"?* As a result, the duo prepared their counterargument. In a nutshell, it was this: "The opportunity presented by the chief was made available to all. We just happened to be the ones who took action. Rank had no bearing on the opportunity to act."

Question #5:

Of all the questions listed here, I think it's safe to assume that most people would feel more comfortable answering this one than the others. In fact, I'm guessing most would answer it this way: "Phil, if I'm going to pitch an idea or initiative that I'm passionate about to decision-makers, of course my primary objective is to get what I want! Otherwise, I'd just be wasting my time."

Jack and Rick felt differently. They weren't interested in wasting time, but just getting what they were pitching was NOT their only objective. They also desired to earn the respect, trust, and ear of ALL executive command staff members, including the chief. If their proposal was developed and presented well, even if rejected, they would still have had the opportunity to build influence with their supervisor and senior colleagues.

Foundational Objectives Prioritized

Two foundational objectives should always be considered whenever working to present ideas and initiatives to decision-makers. They are both exceptionally important, one more so than the other. For the remainder of this book, we will refer to the two objectives as being primary and secondary.

The secondary objective is tricky for some. The reason being, most consider it to be the primary objective in most normal situations. Therefore, some are surprised to learn that "getting what you want" is actually the secondary objective in the *Earning the Right to Be Heard* process.

Let me state clearly that the purpose of this book is to help you get what you want. But helping you get what you want in the short term IS NOT my primary objective. Supporting your long-term success is. Therefore, the primary objective in *Earning the Right to Be Heard* is, in fact, to "earn the right to be heard." In other words, whether you're successful in getting whatever it is you're asking for or not, I still want decision-makers to be interested in what you have to share.

Unlike the would-be students, prospective employees, or individuals in search of mentors like those in the examples given earlier in this chapter, my wish is not for you to lose precious influence as a result of being unprepared and undisciplined. I want you to gain influence—build on it—by way of each and every professional interaction. Remember, gain influence and opportunities follow. Grow opportunities and long-term success is within reach.

Gain influence and opportunities follow. Grow opportunities and long-term success is within reach.

Losing the Right to Be Heard

In the spirit of full disclosure, it's important that we take this opportunity to consider the worst thing that can possibly happen when you go to sell your idea or initiative to decision-makers. What if you were able to get whatever it was that you wanted, yet in the process LOST the right to be heard by decision-makers in the future? Would it be worth it? I doubt it! That could be a disaster. Here's how such a thing could—and does—happen.

Assume for a moment that a particular issue (a.k.a. problem) exists in your department or area of responsibility. It's a known problem that has been present and building over time. This issue extends beyond the bounds of your personal authority to manage it. You can't "fix" it without help from those "higher-up" decision-makers. Frankly, you know it should have—could have—been handled weeks, even months earlier. But for whatever reason—reasons you either don't understand or can't accept but which continue to eat at you—it wasn't.

In the earliest stages of the problem, you casually broached the subject with your manager, suggesting "somebody" (you didn't volunteer to be that person) needed to look into the issue and do something. Your subtle hints subsequently went nowhere. In fact, the problem predictably grew and expanded, thus creating additional problems that have since begun to affect even more people.

With the ever-expanding nature of the problem, grumblings in your area of responsibility have grown. Team members, customers, and vendors alike are beginning to question why you, personally, aren't doing more to resolve the situation.

This should never have happened! you think. *It wouldn't have happened if someone would have done something weeks ago, as I suggested. That's it! I've had all I can take.*

With almost no mental preparation, you storm into the decision-maker's office. Once there, you deliver your ultimatum. Your words and deeds are driven by the passion and emotion of the moment.

Either your boss does what's necessary to resolve this problem once and for all, or you're out. You announce your intention to resign immediately, loudly, in no uncertain terms. You demand to know, "What's it going to be?"

Of course, as you expected, the decision-maker is caught completely flat-footed. There was no way to have predicted this turn of events. He/she quickly evaluates the magnitude of the situation. It's clear that losing you and your expertise on such short notice, at such a critical time, would double the impact of the impending disaster you've just announced. Truth be told, you've done a pretty good job of getting this decision-maker over the "proverbial barrel."

"No, please reconsider," the decision-maker pleads. "I promise to do whatever I can to get this problem reprioritized and resolved as quickly as possible. But I need you to stay with me and see this thing through. I can't afford for you to do anything rash."

It's too late for that. You've already done something rash. You've presented this key decision-maker with an ultimatum. Rash, yes, but was it the smart thing to do? The answer, of course, depends.

It depends on what your identifiable objectives were/are in the present and for the foreseeable future. If your primary, overarching objective was simply to get what you wanted in that moment, regardless of the long-term impact and implications, then congratulations are probably in order. It looks like you will get what it was that you wanted (immediate and definitive action).

But you need to understand that it's also fair to assume that this decision-maker and all other decision-makers who might be privy to your actions of this day will be far better prepared the next time you determine such rash actions are appropriate. Your overly aggressive, heavy-handed approach may work once, this first time. But don't bet on it working two times in a row. Offer a second ultimatum and you may get a formal escort out the front door. Remember the old saying, "Fool me once, shame on you. Fool me twice, shame on me."

Even if a second ultimatum never escapes your mouth, you've most certainly lowered your position in the eyes of the decision-maker. By forcing him/her into a corner and overly emotionalizing the scenario, you've effectively forfeited your influence. Even if your boss doesn't start looking for your replacement immediately following this encounter, you have surely lost your position of authority and respect—you've lost your standing in the organization—unless you can regroup and repair (covered in chapter 13).

Jack and Rick's Postscript

As we prepare to conclude this chapter, there is no intention to leave Rick, Jack, and their proposal in limbo. Inquiring minds want to know: What happened? Did the duo present their proposal to the chief? Was it accepted or rejected? How did other members of the command staff react?

In a nutshell, it turned out just fine for the department and for Jack and Rick. The duo presented their proposal to the chief in a structured way (the specific format to be discussed in chapters to come). After considerable review and months of careful consideration, the plan was accepted and implemented. The chief was pleased with the plan as well as with the plan's originators. Jack and Rick were commended for their initiative and approach, and they both were promoted from their rank as "lowly sergeants" to their new rank as patrol captains (skipping the lieutenant rank altogether). One of the new captains was assigned to oversee the newly designated east section of the community, the other the west.

As for a handful of members of the command staff, yes, predictably, they were upset. "It isn't fair," some argued, "for two young sergeants to get such an opportunity so early and quickly." Luckily for Jack and Rick, they weren't left alone to defend themselves and the decision. The chief did that for them. He explained his decision simply: "Our community policing initiative was a critical one for our department and the community. Everyone knew that. All members of my command staff had equal opportunity to take on this initiative. All were invited to do so. Only two responded. The proposal those two crafted was so detailed and comprehensive, their efforts could not be overlooked. Once the plan was accepted and prepared for implementation, it only made sense to put the plan's originators in place as captains. They created it and proposed it. It was only fair they should have the opportunity to implement it. No one knows it better."

In the remaining parts of this book, you will learn the same approach to selling your ideas as the one successfully implemented by Jack and Rick. Follow the *Earning the Right to Be Heard* process diligently, and you will be well on your way to experiencing the same results as the newly minted captains: you'll learn to better plan for and present your proposals so that you can accomplish your goals, improve your professional standing, and become a trusted colleague whose input is sought by all levels of decision-makers.

A Concise Review

When approaching a decision-maker with an idea you want to sell, do not frame the proposal merely in terms of personal gain or desire. Recognize, respect, and acknowledge the impact it will have on the decision-maker's time, resources, reputation, etc., and highlight the value it will add to others beyond yourself.

Make good impressions and future influence grows, which comes with increased opportunities. Make poor impressions and not only is future influence squandered, but the future opportunities that well-earned influence provides evaporate as well.

Many professionals waste precious resources—the organization's and their own—in pursuit of objectives poorly identified.

The primary objective in *Earning the Right to Be Heard* is securing long-term influence. Secondary is getting what you want in the short term.

SECTION 2:

SETTING THE STAGE

CHAPTER 5

THE FOUNDATION OF INFLUENCE

Intentional Influence

Influence, like beauty, is ultimately determined in "the eye of the beholder." As influence and its impact relate to the *Earning the Right to Be Heard* process, our "beholders" become the buyers of our ideas. In the end, some buyers/decision-makers will be more easily, directly, and predictably influenced than others. But purposefully effecting any sort of influence on the character, development, and behavior of anyone or anything is never a task to be taken lightly. Yet some do. In fact, some people choose to believe that personal influence is little more than some mystical combination of luck, preferential treatment, and fate. For the record, I'm not one of those people. I've learned better. Hopefully, you have (or will) as well.

The relationship you have with key decision-makers in your life six weeks, six months, or six years from now is being shaped by the decisions you make and actions you take in the days to come. Your actions need to be thoughtful and purposeful. Influential relationships are not magical, accidental, or random. Influence grows and expands—or contracts and dies—over time based on criteria that far too many folks deem unimportant or unnecessary. As a result, these same individuals overlook or ignore the necessary criteria altogether. Big mistake. Don't be one of those people.

Intentionally recognizing and fashioning unique interactions with decision-makers in your life can yield a positive, lasting influence on *Earning the Right to Be Heard*. It is the "secret sauce" to ensuring this influence-building process progresses smoothly—the glue that holds the system together. That's why, before we get into the specific steps for *Earning the Right to Be Heard*, it is crucial that we cover the five primary criteria for establishing a good rapport with decision-makers.

The Five C's of Influence

Various criteria are involved in the growth and advancement of one's influence—certainly more than I have room here to explore adequately. But there are at least five specific criteria that effectively support the *Earning the Right to Be Heard* process: connection, communication, credibility, commitment, and curiosity.

Connection

Connection is unquestionably key to influence-building. Without solid connection between idea sellers and decision-makers, little hope exists for the advancement of even the most worthwhile ideas and initiatives. To get things done, sellers and buyers must pull in the same direction. Connection enables that pulling process to begin.

Connections can occur organically based on criteria such as physical proximity, shared interests, personality alignment—or something else entirely. From the perspective of the *Earning the Right to Be Heard* process, the most favorable way to connect with and influence decision-makers is through the identification of a shared challenge (a.k.a. problem), the unmistakable ability to "understand that challenge" and "talk the same language," and some observable preparation in tackling the challenge. It's from such a foundation that substantive conversations take place and connections are made.

Because the idea seller voluntarily introduces the idea, the responsibility for establishing the initial connection always rests with him/her. More plainly stated, the person initiating the *Earning the Right to Be Heard* interaction is the one responsible for assuring the idea is appropriately communicated to and received by decision-makers.

Communication

Closely related to connection is the critical need to communicate proactively and effectively. Think of the relationship between connection and communication this way: if no connection between parties has been

> To get things done, sellers and buyers must pull in the same direction.

established, then effective communication is an impossibility. At best, communicative efforts under such disconnected circumstances are superficial. At worst, communication shuts down completely.

Once connection has been established, the idea seller must manage the elements that contribute to the communication scenario to the best of their ability. By anticipating (and mitigating/eliminating) potential barriers that could derail their efforts and catering their message and delivery to the demands of the communication scenario, the idea seller can increase the chances that their message will be well received. The four broad categories into which possible barriers fall include *sender barriers*, *receiver barriers*, *message barriers*, and *environmental barriers*.

Sender Barriers

Sender barriers always originate with the idea "sender" (seller). Conceivably, they become the easiest of all barriers to mitigate or avoid entirely since the sender controls them completely. A sampling of sender barriers discussed in this book include unbridled emotion, lack of advance thought and/or preparation, and poor communication of intent. The good news is each of these can be managed appropriately, and you'll learn how to do so in this book. Broader sender barriers include inconsistent actions (not meeting expectations), inappropriate messaging (inconsistent verbal and nonverbal communication), and failure to deliver (lack of follow-up and promises kept). These pages contain "work-arounds" for these issues as well.

Receiver Barriers

Receiver barriers focus on the decision-maker's (the buyer's) inability to effectively receive your idea for consideration. For the seller, some receiver barriers are easier to recognize and, therefore, manage than others. For example, idea sellers might anticipate a decision-maker's unfavorable reaction to a particular presentation methodology, environmental distractions, verbiage, or even the idea seller's physical appearance. It goes to reason that if a receiver barrier can be anticipated, it should be addressed (eliminated) in advance. Other receiver barriers may be harder to manage, such as a decision maker's wandering mind, poor listening skills, or fundamental disinterest in the topic. These may be harder to manage, but they should never be ignored.

Message Barriers

Message barriers exist within the content of the communicated idea or initiative itself. They include lack of clarity and/or coherence, incomplete or superfluous information, perceived lack of relevance, and unsubstantiated claims. Because they create the message, idea sellers are also responsible for overcoming these barriers. As an idea seller, you must remember that this is your meeting; you are responsible for the clarity of the message. The essence of your message must be immediately apparent and its relevance to the decision-maker foregrounded. To that end, the ageless advice of one of history's greatest deliverers of critical messaging, Winston Churchill, should be helpful: "If you have an important point to make, don't try to be subtle or clever. Use a pile driver. Hit the point once. Then come back and hit again. Then hit it a third time."

Environmental Barriers

The fourth and final category of barriers is admittedly a "catchall." It includes all the factors that can affect a communication scenario that are not exclusively related to the idea sender, idea receiver, or message—in other words, context and culture. Environmental barriers include the timing of the message; historical or contemporary issues (social, economic, etc.), both inside and outside the organization, that might affect how the message is delivered and/or received; company culture (e.g., lack of openness from leadership to change); and the medium in which the message is delivered (e.g., technology hiccups, inaccessibility of the message).

Regardless of the category or categories into which a particular barrier falls, the burden of building and maintaining connection remains with the idea seller. Therefore, in preparation, idea sellers should routinely ask—and answer—this question: *What might cause my presentation to the decision-maker to fail?* Ask the question of yourself; then work diligently to identify every conceivable answer to that question. Remember, a question well asked is generally a problem half solved. Or said a different way: if a barrier can be imagined, solutions can usually be crafted to mitigate or eliminate its ill effects.

Credibility

Establishing personal credibility is one of the premier ways to build personal influence with decision-makers. Period. Remember that fundamentally, credibility is nothing more than having others trust and believe in you and what you're telling them.

Therefore, credibility (trust and belief) may grow from what sellers purposefully *tell* decision-makers about their educational backgrounds, depth of knowledge, past experiences, unique skill sets, and so forth. But credibility grows more

> A question well asked is generally a problem half solved.

quickly and surely when individuals both *tell* and *show* that they can be trusted and believed.

Visual demonstration is incredibly important to having decision-makers trust and believe in you and your message. Both must be congruent. Telling and showing must be aligned. In order for decision-makers to trust and believe the message, they must first trust and believe the messenger.

In my former life as a corporate human resources manager, I interviewed many prospective employees. Of course, I paid close attention to what a candidate's resume or application "told" me about his/her education, skills, and past experiences. But I paid even closer attention to what the candidate "showed" me during the face-to-face interview: hygiene, mode of dress, personal presence, attention to detail, professional demeanor, interactions with others, thoughtful answers for difficult questions, and so on. Whenever a disconnect occurred between what I had been told and what I saw, it had to be reconciled before I could comfortably move forward in the hiring process.

The same concept applies to the dynamic between idea sellers and those who will commit to buying those ideas. If you tell a decision-maker you're willing to do "whatever it takes" to make your initiative a success, it helps immensely if you've demonstrated that "will do" attitude previously. But if all they've seen is you talking a good game, then shrinking from and griping about new responsibilities when assigned, you shouldn't be surprised if the decision-maker is less than enthusiastic about your idea.

The *Earning the Right to Be Heard* process is rooted in foundational demonstration: showing how an idea or initiative can be accomplished, illustrating the benefits that the idea or initiative can produce, and tying it all together with a credible messenger—one who can be trusted and believed explicitly.

Commitment

Credibility goes hand in hand with the fourth C—commitment. This criterion requires personal involvement. You can claim to be committed to an ideal, but if you are not personally engaged, with little to no skin in the game, it's difficult, if not impossible, to impress upon others the significance of your personal influence. On the other hand, if you're in the arena striving to make a difference, that causes decision-makers to take notice and grant you more authority.

The *Earning the Right to Be Heard* process is built, start to finish, on the foundation of personal commitment by individuals. Individuals committed to identifying things that can be made better. Individuals willing to get their hands dirty with the tasks of investigating, researching, and formulating plans to support improvement initiatives. Even more obvious, individuals willing to step up, stand up, and speak up for what they believe. Yes, commitment is evident and critical in every stage of the *Earning the Right to Be Heard* process.

Note that the suggestions you make should never sound or look more like complaints than solutions. Commitment requires that you don't point fingers, but rather solve problems. Decision-makers pay attention to that level of commitment. At its core, *Earning the Right to Be Heard* represents a personal commitment to doing all you can to be an invested contributor to those causes that will benefit the organization and those whom the organization serves.

Curiosity

The fifth criterion for building influence with decision-makers is curiosity. When used properly, the *Earning the Right to Be Heard* process is mobilized by, and generates, curiosity—both on the part of the idea seller and the decision-maker. For this reason, curiosity serves as an idea seller's consistent ally, as well as a powerful motivator for decision-makers. Here's why.

Without delving too deeply into the neuroscience of curiosity, know that researchers have determined that curiosity of almost any sort creates an immediate state of mental, emotional, and biological arousal. In other words, when curious, our minds, psyches, and bodies literally change and remain in a state of flux until our curiosity is satisfied.

From the moment you approach a decision-maker with a developed idea, you subtly communicate that you know, understand, and are in possession of something worthy of knowing—but something of which they are not yet aware. That state of not knowing creates immediate curiosity, as well as the intrinsic arousal that accompanies it.

Once curiosity has been aroused, the decision-maker predictably, almost involuntarily, is motivated to engage in exploration intended to reduce his/her state of mental arousal. In other words, decision-makers will have questions. They will necessarily seek answers to their questions. If your information-sharing process of choice (*Earning the Right to Be Heard*) supplies them with the answers they need, they can be expected, compelled even, to remain engaged with you for the duration of the process—that is, until their questions are answered and their curiosity quelled. Thereby, as mentioned before, curiosity is your ally—your friend.

In the next chapter, exploration of the various steps of the *Earning the Right to Be Heard* process begins in earnest. The goal is to build a state of perpetual curiosity into the process for the decision-maker from the outset. You will be shown how to approach a decision-maker to request an initial meeting. That simple request is designed to trigger a curiosity response from the decision-maker—one that will continue for the duration of the process—thus enabling you to start strong and maintain momentum.

A Concise Review

Influential relationships are not magical, accidental, or random. Influence grows and expands—or contracts and dies—over time based on criteria that far too many folks deem to be unimportant or unnecessary.

The five primary criteria for establishing a good rapport with decision-makers are connection, communication, credibility, commitment, and curiosity.

The *Earning the Right to Be Heard* process is rooted in foundational demonstration: showing how an idea or initiative can be accomplished, illustrating the benefits that the idea or initiative can produce, and tying it all together with a credible messenger—one who can be trusted and believed explicitly.

Suggestions you make should never sound or look more like complaints than solutions. Commitment requires that you don't point fingers, but rather solve problems.

Once curiosity has been aroused, the decision-maker is motivated to engage in exploration intended to reduce his/her state of mental stimulation. In other words, decision-makers will have questions. They will necessarily seek answers to their questions.

CHAPTER 6

STARTING STRONG

The Risk Reward

The previous chapter explored the various aspects of what makes personal influence most effective: professional connection, communication, credibility, commitment, and curiosity in appropriate combination. In this chapter and those to follow, that personal influence will be put to the test. Specifically, it will be directed toward selling this worthwhile idea of yours. Remember, for your personal influence to be most effective, its use must be intentional, logical, and sequential.

Shortly, you will learn the first step in the process is to request a formal meeting with the decision-maker. This meeting's purpose will be to introduce your idea formally. Like every other step in the process, it should not be taken lightly or for granted. It requires thought, planning, and yes, a bit of courage. After all, there are many who might wish to do what you are preparing to do—but simply can't make themselves move forward. That's where the courage to think and act in new ways necessarily comes into play.

Niccolò Machiavelli, an Italian author and politician, recognized the inherent hesitancy men and women experience in tackling new objectives. His quote, written approximately 500 years ago, still rings true today: "There is nothing more difficult to take in hand, more perilous to conduct, or more uncertain in its success, than to take the lead in the introduction of a new order of things."

For many reading this book, beginning the *Earning the Right to Be Heard* process truly marks a new approach or a "new order of things." However, just because something new and different might appear to be "difficult," "perilous," and initially "uncertain," that does not mean it is absent opportunity, merit, or even growth. In fact, quite the opposite. As the English poet T. S. Eliot acknowledged, "Only those who risk going too far will see how far they can go." It is my belief that this process, when successfully implemented, can take you farther than you have gone to date—and even farther than you might imagine. You have the opportunity now to start strong.

First Steps

The following offers an example of what starting strong looks like for the *Earning the Right to Be Heard* process. You might use it as a model for your own first steps into the process. Imagine the interaction was initiated by an employee, Brenda, and directed to one of her organization's key decision-makers, Mr. Malek. The process is set in motion once Brenda approaches the decision-maker unannounced.

(BEGIN INTERACTION)

"Good morning, Mr. Malek. Have you got a minute?"

"Sure, Brenda. What's up?"

"Mr. Malek, I'd like to schedule a meeting with you sometime soon. When would you have 30 minutes to share?"

(Confused, Mr. Malek responds.)

"For what, Brenda?"

"There's something I've been working on that I believe has significant benefit for the organization. I'd like time to share my thoughts with you."

(PAUSE INTERACTION)

Okay, let's stop here and do a quick debriefing.

How many times might you expect to overhear (or engage in) a conversation like the one depicted here? Weekly? Monthly? Ever?

I'm guessing your response might be, "Seldom, if ever."

It's more common for a decision-maker to schedule an unexpected meeting with a team member than the other way around. That's exactly why this first stage of this simple yet powerful technique is so important to understand and to properly implement.

The decision-maker is certain to be curious about your approach, the topic, and of course, its ultimate significance. Questions regarding each can (and will) play in your favor eventually—but only if you anticipate, prepare for, and play them right. Be ready.

(RESUME INTERACTION)

> "Sounds interesting, Brenda. I've got some time. We can talk now."

(PAUSE INTERACTION)

It's official. Mr. Malek's curiosity has been piqued.

However, this is a VERY IMPORTANT point. Brenda MUST resist the temptation of being pulled into this conversation at this moment. She's not yet fully prepared, and neither is Mr. Malek. The initial meeting must be delayed until Brenda is ready to present her idea with her established logic and rationale. Unusual as it might seem to say "no" in that moment, it's necessary. Brenda's proper response should be:

(RESUME INTERACTION)

> "Thanks, Mr. Malek, I appreciate your immediate availability. But I'm not quite finished compiling the information for your review. Today I'm just asking for 30 minutes on your calendar. Anything available?"

> "How about Wednesday at 10:30 a.m., Brenda?"

> "Perfect! I'll be ready by then. Thanks."

(INITIAL INTERACTION CONCLUDED)

Now that wasn't so hard, was it? Starting strong is really as simple as that.

With the initial meeting scheduled, it's time for Brenda to turn her full attention to the rest of the steps in the *Earning the Right to Be Heard* process. Full and proper preparation will be key to her success moving forward. We'll continue to explore those preparatory steps in the chapters to follow.

A Concise Review

For personal influence to be most effective, its use must be intentional, logical, and sequential. From the beginning of the process to its logical conclusion, the opportunity to influence something or someone—the capacity to affect behavior or outcomes in some way—should never be taken for granted, squandered, or abused.

The decision-maker is certain to be curious about your approach, the topic, and of course, its significance. Questions regarding each can (and will) play in your favor eventually—but only if you anticipate, prepare for, and play them right now.

Pique a decision-maker's curiosity about your idea or issue by alerting them to your desire to set a meeting time with them. Always set it for the future, even if they offer to meet right away.

CHAPTER 7

OPENING STATEMENTS

Time Is Money

The previous chapter ended with a meeting requested and scheduled with a decision-maker. The stated purpose of that meeting was to share an idea Brenda had personally been thinking about and working on. It's important to note that this self-initiated idea was presented to this decision-maker as one having significant potential benefit to the organization.

With this "starting" example available, it should be easy enough to recognize the necessary steps for requesting and scheduling your own first meeting. With the formal scheduling of a meeting, your first *Earning the Right to Be Heard* process step will be officially underway. We now must continue preparations and pave the way for additional influence opportunities that are sure to follow.

Let's assume you've now been granted 30 minutes of your decision-maker's precious time. In reality, a full 30 minutes may not be necessary to present your idea. Commit to never squandering a single minute of the time entrusted to you.

First-year business students understand the "time is money" consideration. Dedication and discipline in managing time wisely are hallmarks of conscientious professionals and the *Earning the Right to Be Heard* process. Business operators and decision-makers quickly determine whether or not they can trust *your* judgment in large part by the way you manage *their* time. Therefore, the next step of this process allows you the opportunity to prove their time is safe in your hands.

They Know a Thing or Two

A few years ago, a series of television commercials promoting an American insurance company that specializes in automobile accident coverage was very popular. These creative Farmers Insurance advertisements humorously depict unusual automobile accidents and the company's composed handling of them. The more outlandish the accidents, the more engaging the commercial. In fact, each commercial highlights an accident so bizarre it supposedly earned induction into Farmers' fictitious "Hall of Claims."

These 30- to 60-second promotions are clever, entertaining, and effective. Based on the premise that most accidents are basically fender benders, the extreme examples depicted indirectly communicate a "you can trust us with

Commit to never squandering a single minute of the time entrusted to you.

your vehicle in every situation" vibe. But in case the hyperbolic approach doesn't work, taking no chances, each commercial drives the point home with the powerful catchphrase: "We know a thing or two, because we've seen a thing or two."

That's an important point for all of us to remember when preparing to present our ideas to seasoned decision-makers. The person about to be addressed is undoubtedly experienced, knowledgeable, and trusted. The decision-makers with whom you will be interacting most certainly "know a thing or two, because they've seen a thing or two." They should be treated as such.

But you know a thing or two, too. More importantly, at the moment, you actually know something the decision-maker doesn't—something you've promised to share with them. You possess an idea that is supported by the "power of curiosity." Exercise great caution. Never waste available time, opportunity, or curiosity from the meeting's first moment on.

Creative Ownership

There is much to be prepared before the first minute of the initial meeting. Specifically, you must prepare a formal introduction of the initiative; research, collect, and collate necessary support materials (proofs); anticipate the decision-maker's questions; and develop solid responses to each of those questions. That's quite a bit of preparation. But that preparation will serve you well, and it will signal to the decision-maker that you are serious.

It's imperative to remember this is a meeting YOU have requested, a meeting in which YOU will define the working objectives, a meeting for which YOU alone will prepare, and ultimately a meeting during which

YOU must assume primary leadership responsibility. This is a big deal. Don't underestimate that reality. Managed well, the meeting has the potential to change the trajectory of your career. Managed poorly, the negative aftereffects (including reduced influence) can linger long in the decision-maker's mind.

Don't be frightened by such bold pronouncements. You should, however, fully appreciate and accept this wonderful opportunity for what it is. Too often people are shortsighted, unable to see past the immediate challenge to the longer-term opportunity.

When individuals focus solely on the challenge, questions naturally arise along with those dreaded doubts. Inevitably, individuals will question their (as of yet) untested and unproven ability to successfully apply the principles contained in the *Earning the Right to Be Heard* process. Sadly, while in the throes of momentary, fleeting doubt, a few easily discouraged souls will opt to abandon the process altogether, doing so even before testing it sufficiently to see if will work for them or not.

Bad idea. Don't let that person be you.

You have formulated this idea, this initiative. You must now take complete ownership of it. As its "creative owner," you are the most prepared and best-positioned individual to lead the way in advancing its cause. Therefore, it's inconceivable, impractical, and frankly, irresponsible to consider shrinking from this important task. It is time to commit to seeing it through from invention to implementation by giving it life through the *Earning the Right to Be Heard* process.

The moment has come to accept your personal responsibility. The time is now to take legitimate ownership and action. You are the rightful creative owner who wishes to see this idea, this initiative, develop to full bloom. As its creative owner, you are the best person for the job of describing, detailing, and defending it.

Self-Inflicted Wounds

Now that you have committed to following through with ALL aspects of the *Earning the Right to Be Heard* process, your attention must turn completely to preparing for the scheduled meeting. Specifically, BEFORE that meeting you will need to be completely ready with the following:

3 Opening Statements

5 Questions—5 Answers

The balance of this chapter is dedicated to providing specific "how" and "why" support in order to prepare for and properly introduce those three opening statements. The five questions and their corresponding answers will be introduced and explored in the chapters that immediately follow. Welcome to the heart of the *Earning the Right to Be Heard* process.

If scheduling the initial meeting was handled properly (as outlined in the previous chapter), it's reasonable to expect the decision-maker's curiosity to be significant. The decision-maker is sure to have wondered repeatedly 1) what the meeting would be about, 2) how it would be managed, and finally 3) what might be expected of him/her.

Adhering closely to the formal elements of the *Earning the Right to Be Heard* process should satiate the decision-maker's curiosity, while also highlighting your meeting management skills and establishing clear expectations for future decisions and actions.

Now don't shoot yourself in the foot.

I wish I had a dollar for every meeting I've attended in my career that started the wrong way, thus getting me and the other participants off on the wrong foot. I'd be richer still if I had a quarter for every eye roll, heavy sigh, body shift, and/or impatient twitch I've observed when attendees involuntarily reacted to meetings that started (and usually continued) the wrong way. If so, I'd be a wealthy man. But if you're the unlucky one who is guilty of starting meetings the wrong way, it is you who will pay the price.

Failing is never the goal. But failing before you've even begun the process is simply intolerable, especially when it's within your capacity to control and influence the meeting from beginning to end—the first minute to the last. To do otherwise results in what should be considered "avoidable failures," which generally result in "self-inflected wounds," with lasting scars to remind you of them.

No Small Talk

To start this first, most important meeting properly, small talk must not be allowed to derail the conversation. In social situations, small talk is appropriate, even desirable. It "breaks the ice" and "gets people to relax." In a business setting, small talk usually has the unintended opposite effect.

When a meeting begins on the wrong foot, participants can easily experience initial confusion followed by growing frustration, then tension. Most people won't voice their frustration publicly, but that doesn't stop the tension from coloring their thoughts about the person allowing it to occur—you.

I'm not against discussing sports scores, the weather, or even updated sales forecasts. But now is not the time. This meeting should be singularly focused on the idea/initiative you are presenting to the decision-maker for consideration. You can't knowingly afford to let anything detract from your stated objectives.

When meetings begin with off-topic conversations, two bad things are bound to happen—and usually quickly. First, time is sure to be wasted. Frankly, after such a distraction we may never be able to regain the proper tone again. That's not only a waste; it's a shame—a missed opportunity.

But wasted time is not the only concern. With every minute of time wasted via small talk and off-topic conversation, hard-earned personal influence dwindles away as well.

"If he/she can't manage this meeting," decision-makers may think, "how can I trust him/her to manage something as important as the project in question?"

The main problem with small talk is that it has nothing to do with your stated objectives. Please realize and accept that allowing even a couple of minutes of unnecessary small talk can be exponentially counterproductive to your purposes. Any unrelated topic introduced into *your* meeting—especially at the start—detracts unnecessarily from its purpose and therefore weakens *your* position of influence.

Start Strong

Once the appointed time for the meeting arrives and the participants are in place, the moment has come for you to step up and lead. It's time to let your preparation shine.

This IS NOT the time for you to ease tentatively out of the starting gate. This IS the time for you to bolt from the starting gate, eyes fixed determinedly on the finish line. Moving quickly and intentionally does not require a brash, arrogant, off-putting manner. Instead, your intentionality should be indicative of a confident, poised, prepared persona.

In a meeting of this type, it's best to start strong with a concise opening statement. I suggest three sentences work best. Each sentence is carefully crafted to communicate a specific message.

Opening Statement/Sentence #1:

Clearly and specifically state what you want.

Opening Statement/Sentence #2:

Clearly and specifically state why you want it.

Opening Statement/Sentence #3:

Clearly and specifically state your readiness for and openness to addressing any and all questions that the decision-maker(s) will certainly have.

Working in tandem, the three statements should flow as follows:

> **(Statement #1)** "Mr./Mrs. (BLANK #1), thank you again for your time today. I'm here to request (BLANK #2).

(Statement #2) Personally, I'm convinced the time has come for us to carefully consider committing organizational resources to addressing the critical issue of (BLANK #3).

(Statement #3) Therefore, I've come prepared to answer your questions regarding this specific request."

The anonymity of the three "blanks" indicates a fluid process that can be applied to a meeting with any **PERSON** (**BLANK #1**), for the purpose of proposing any **ACTION** (**BLANK #2**), to solve an identified **ISSUE** (**BLANK #3**). Even once the respective "BLANKS" have been appropriately filled in, the opening statement should be under 50 words. It should easily take less than 30 seconds to deliver those three sentences.

In other words, it doesn't take long to get a well-planned meeting started, communicate your intentions, and create a positive first impression. Due to your professional start, it's fair to expect other meeting participant(s) to be more engaged from the outset.

As for experienced decision-makers, who are professionally trained to recognize the "time is money" concept, they are sure to be favorably impressed. Using less than a single minute of their time for such a focused opening sends the unmistakable, albeit subliminal messages: "this person *means* business," "this person *knows* business," and "this person *deserves* my utmost attention."

Having a well-developed opening statement is a critical first step in *Earning the Right to Be Heard* and getting what you want. But we're not there yet. Next come the critical steps of anticipating and answering the questions that trained decision-makers are certain to have for you.

A Concise Review

It's imperative to remember this is a meeting YOU requested... for which YOU have prepared...and for which YOU must assume primary responsibility for leading.

Decision-makers quickly determine whether or not they can trust *your* judgment in large part by the way you manage *their* time.

Small talk is often seen as an effort to "break the ice" and "get people to relax," but more often it has an opposite, unintended effect.

The best way to start strong is with a concise opening statement:

- Sentence #1: Clearly and specifically state what it is that you want.

- Sentence #2: Clearly and specifically state why you want it.

- Sentence #3: Clearly and specifically state your readiness for and openness to addressing any and all questions that the decision-maker(s) will certainly have.

CHAPTER 8

FIVE KEY QUESTIONS

Questions Propel Learning

Former professional mixed martial artist Georges St-Pierre is quoted as having said, "The more knowledge you get, the more questions you ask. The smarter you get, the more you realize that everything is possible."

I agree with Mr. St-Pierre on every point made—and not just because it makes sense to stay on his good side. In fact, Mr. St-Pierre's philosophy aligns nicely with the *The Question Continuum* introduced earlier in chapter 1. You may recall that a process was introduced while discussing "Sellers and Buyers." This cyclical process occurs once individuals give themselves permission to ask those questions that most need to be answered. The continuum was depicted in the following construct:

The Question Continuum

QUESTIONS PROPEL LEARNING;

LEARNING FUELS ADVANCEMENT;

ADVANCEMENT BUILDS INFLUENCE;

INFLUENCE GROWS OPPORTUNITIES; AND

OPPORTUNITIES INCREASE QUESTIONS.

Notice the entire process starts and ends—or in reality, loops—with questions. Questions are destined to propel—accelerate—learning. Ask the right questions and conceivably any problem is already half solved. Becoming adept at asking good questions allows us all to learn and advance—to move forward, accepting new challenges as we go.

Then as we go and grow, our personal and professional advancement naturally provides fertile ground for influence to take root, which leads inevitably to new and expanding opportunities. As this process moves along, we once again find ourselves back at the beginning of the continuum with new, more advanced questions.

The significant difference the second (and third, fourth, fifth) time around the continuum is that different questions are asked, each time deeper and more nuanced, thereby leading to elevated levels of understanding, expertise, and individual performance. But again, it all hinges on questions.

The major advancements were, are, and always will be driven by what was learned and experienced from the questions that were asked and the answers that followed. The best decision-makers know (and practice) that. Great decision-makers, therefore, are ultimately great question-askers—and more. Celebrity chef Anne Burrell revealed the "and more" when she said, "Part of being successful is about asking questions *and* listening to the answers." Idea sellers, for their part, must be committed question-askers and listeners as well.

Patience Is a Virtue

Now that you understand that questions are not an affront, but rather an opportunity to advance your position, you can engage in the *Earning the Right to Be Heard* process without fear of allowing your emotions to thwart your intentions. If you're still a bit uneasy, that's to be expected the first few times you employ the process. Just know that patience is truly a virtue from this point forward. Trust the process. Don't allow your passion for the idea and your emotions in the moment to undercut your efforts. How you respond to the decision-maker's questions is a critical part of *Earning the Right to Be Heard* and, hopefully, securing what it is you're asking for.

It's a common refrain from individuals who've attempted—and failed—to sell some important idea to blame the decision-maker. They seldom grasp the real reason why a decision-maker won't give them (and their respective idea) more time, attention, and support. Idea sellers are too often painfully unaware of their own level of ignorance (lack of knowledge, information, or understanding) regarding the decision-making process. They don't know what they don't know. However, this foundational ignorance is often uncomfortably obvious to decision-makers.

So, what is it that decision-makers see that idea sellers often overlook? Four lethal components: passion without logic, emotion without reason, presentation without preparation, and questions without answers. In isolation, each component is certainly a challenge to be overcome. But in virtually any combination, the four can devastate a seller's chances of positively influencing any decision-maker. Consequently, with the demise of the good idea, so go immediate prospects for *Earning the Right to Be Heard* and any opportunities that might have followed.

Having conducted postmortems on failed idea presentations, I've often heard frustrated sellers voice the following:

"I've got an idea that would be great for the organization. But the decision-maker is clueless. When I cornered him and told him specifically what needs to be done, all he seemed interested in was asking me questions. If I had trouble answering even one of his questions, our conversation stopped right there. I'd have to find the answer before he was willing to talk again. He's just stalling! I'm over it!"

Sound familiar? Probably.

First, in trying to understand the idea seller's frustration, consider the last statement first. Do you really believe s/he's "over it"? I don't. There is just too much raw emotion evident to assume s/he's ready to forget and move on.

Second, do you believe the decision-maker is "stalling"? I don't. Professional decision-makers are always searching for good ideas. Historically, questions are the foundational tool decision-makers use to determine the legitimacy of ideas being considered.

Third, do you believe the decision-maker is "clueless"? Again, I don't. Any "cornered" decision-maker should be expected to ask pointed questions for the purpose of clarification and information-gathering. No decision-maker worth his or her salt would do less.

So, do you believe there might be an opportunity our frustrated idea seller has overlooked? I do. In fact, the idea seller admitted as much:

"If I had trouble answering one of his questions, our conversation would stop right there. I'd be sent away to find the answer before he was willing to talk again."

There it is. Apparently, while engulfed in the emotion of the moment, the team member inadvertently misinterpreted the real purpose of the decision-maker's questions. The questions were not meant to dismiss or reject the request out of hand. Rather, the questions created an opportunity for the idea seller to prepare and deliver complete and sufficient answers—answers that might justify the request outright. Therefore, questions are good.

Charting the Flow

Every coin has two sides. Therefore, to get a true picture of the nature of most any challenge, it's advisable to step back and evaluate the challenge from both sides and as many different angles as possible.

With this question challenge, we know there are two active participants—an idea seller and a decision-maker. Both parties know the decision-maker holds the upper hand—the power to grant, withhold, or withdraw support of the idea in question. Nothing the idea seller may pitch will occur without the tacit support and formal approval of the decision-maker in charge.

Therefore, enabling the idea seller to view the current challenge through the eyes of the decision-maker could be exceptionally helpful. Seeing the world through the other person's eyes allows the next right steps to reveal themselves. Think of it as the equivalent of playing a card game where one player knows what cards his/her playing partner needs. With that knowledge, the cards in the partner's hand are played accordingly.

In *Earning the Right to Be Heard*, the other party, the decision-maker, is not our opponent but rather a team member, our partner. As team members working toward the same goal, we should work to understand and complement one another, realizing victory ultimately benefits both parties.

Way back in my college days, I took an introductory class in basic computer programming. Honestly, I remember almost nothing from that class, with one single exception. That class introduced me to "flowcharting" as a form of decision-making.

Admittedly, I still know little about the technical aspects of flowchart design. But what I do know has been helpful to me over the years. The use of a flowchart to diagram *Earning the Right to Be Heard* as a working process may be helpful to you as well. It should offer a clearer understanding of how decision-makers are trained to think.

In the spirit of simplicity, the next two pages are designed to allow you the opportunity to review and familiarize yourself with, first, the flowchart shapes, symbols, and meanings, then the flowchart diagram design itself. But relax! I promise to keep it exceptionally simple—and practical. It's intended to be a helpful visual aid in guiding your future *Earning the Right to Be Heard* preparation, progress, and success.

Understanding the Meaning of the Shapes

In the world of flowchart design, each shape visually depicts a different action. For our purposes, there are only four shapes to remember.

This shape indicates a defined process, task, action, or operation to follow.

This shape indicates the point of entry (start) of a process
and the point of exit (end) of a process.

This shape indicates an action which must be accomplished.

This shape indicates a question to be asked to determine a specific decision.
(Yes/No? Stop/Go?)

Earning the Right to Be Heard Flowchart

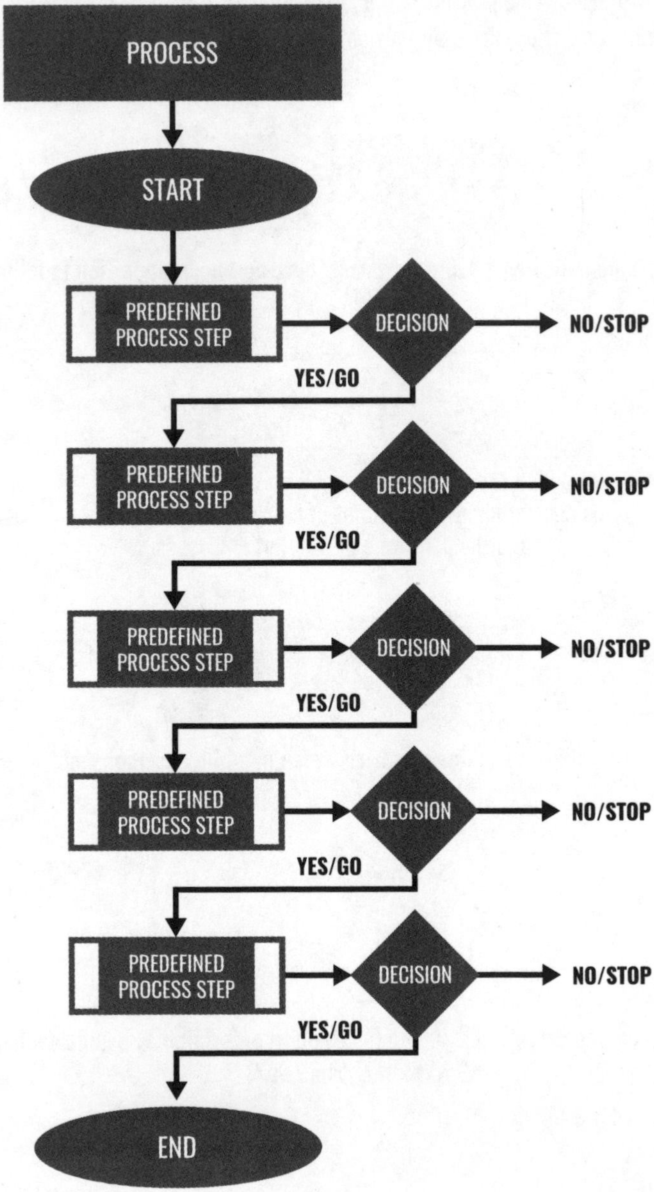

Earning the Right to Be Heard Flowchart / Step by Step

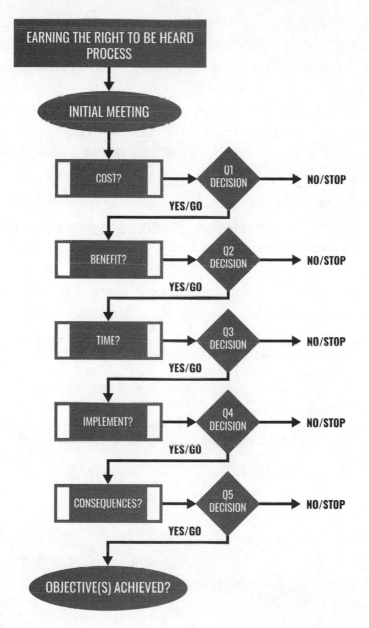

Five Key Questions

As pictured in the flowchart just introduced, five "predefined process points" constitute the heart of our *Earning the Right to Be Heard* process. Each of these process points is represented by a specific question. No legitimate decision-maker can professionally justify his/her decision without first having answers to these questions. Therefore, for you to successfully "sell" your idea, you MUST be able to answer the five key questions to the decision-maker's (buyer's) satisfaction. It's that simple.

The next five chapters of this book are dedicated to exploring those five key questions. The importance of recognizing, preparing for, and appropriately addressing these five questions simply cannot be overemphasized. Good decision-makers can't make informed decisions (and therefore, be considered good decision-makers) without asking, then evaluating, the responses to these five key questions. They are that important.

To eliminate unnecessary suspense, these upcoming five questions are:

- Question #1: The COST?

- Question #2: The BENEFIT?

- Question #3: The TIME?

- Question #4: The IMPLEMENTATION?

- Question #5: The CONSEQUENCE?

Each question will be explored thoroughly in its respective chapter. We will do a deep dive into each question, including both appropriate and inappropriate responses. But there is at least one other consideration that needs to be noted before we direct our attention exclusively to the five questions.

Sequence Happens

There is a particular sequence to be expected and planned for regarding the order in which these five questions will normally be asked. You are well-advised to be ready for that sequence. Namely, Question #1: The COST Question and Question #2: The BENEFIT Question will almost always be asked in that order.

Occasionally, some exuberant training participant will challenge this established order. Their argument is that if the benefit of some decision/action is great enough or important enough, the cost of that decision should be a secondary or lesser consideration. It's a good academic argument. However, we're not functioning in a classroom here. This is the real work world; therefore, arguing over the proper order of the cost/benefit questions becomes an unnecessary waste of time. Decision-makers en masse have long since determined that "cost" trumps "benefits" in most early-stage considerations.

That's not to say that benefits should be ignored as a selling point. Two chapters from now, you will learn the great importance of benefits well established and specifically communicated. But, as a rule of thumb, if you can't successfully answer the "cost" question when first asked, don't expect the "benefit" question to see the light of day. So again, "cost" will be Question #1, followed by "benefit" as Question #2.

That leaves Question #3: The TIME Question; Question #4: The IMPLEMENTATION Question; and Question #5: The CONSEQUENCE Question as questions to follow. Unlike Questions #1 and #2, I'm less certain about the order of these three questions. The final sequence will end up being a point of personal preference for each individual decision-maker.

Often these three additional questions arise naturally from discussion of other questions previously asked. As decision-makers consider and evaluate the acceptability of your answers to initial questions, they naturally become more curious and want to know more. Expect that. That's a good thing.

Therefore, you MUST be prepared with responses for ALL five questions at all times. DO NOT schedule the initial meeting with the decision-maker unless you're prepared with answers for all five questions. To do otherwise puts the entire process at risk. You never want to be caught off guard and unable to answer a predictable question when asked, regardless of what order the questions may come.

A Concise Review

Questions are foundational tools that decision-makers use to determine the legitimacy of ideas under consideration.

Questions are destined to propel—accelerate—learning. Ask the right questions and conceivably any problem is already half solved.

Failure of the *Earning the Right to Be Heard* process generally results from a potent combination of passion without logic, emotion without reason, presentation without preparation—plus questions without answers.

Five "predetermined process points" constitute the heart of our *Earning the Right to Be Heard* process, each represented by a specific question:

- Question #1: The COST?

- Question #2: The BENEFIT?

- Question #3: The TIME?

- Question #4: The IMPLEMENTATION?

- Question #5: The CONSEQUENCE?

No legitimate decision-maker can justify his/her decision without first having satisfactory answers to these questions.

CHAPTER 9

HOW MUCH WILL IT COST?

A Critical Juncture

This chapter marks a critical juncture in the execution of the *Earning the Right to Be Heard* process. By now you've read, thought, and reasoned your way through the book's first two sections: *Understanding the Concept* and *Setting the Stage*. If so, you're most likely already enjoying residual benefits from the exercise—benefits that may include, but are certainly not limited to, being awarded more personal respect, more professional regard, and more of the precious "ear" of decision-makers.

That's a good place to be and a promising point from which to proceed. It signals that decision-makers are aware of the mental acuity, the intentional preparation, and the professional awareness that support the effort associated with selling any worthwhile initiative.

But getting to the starting line is not what *Earning the Right to Be Heard* is about. The anticipated payoff associated with this (or any) worthwhile effort (i.e., a plan envisioned, a project proposed, an undertaking begun) waits at the finish line.

How Much Will It Cost?

As your requested meeting with the decision-maker approaches, your adrenalin should be pumping. You may be a little "keyed up." Your mind/body connection is sure to sense the importance of this professional interaction. But relax. You'll be prepared. Just view this as the valuable opportunity that it is—then continue to prepare aggressively and appropriately for it.

By the way, your decision-maker of choice has been thinking about this meeting, too. Since the moment you formally requested it, his/her curiosity has remained piqued. This is a relatively new experience for him/her, as well. Team members don't normally request such meetings.

It's all moving forward as intended. Just trust the process. As the meeting time arrives and begins, consciously and intentionally skip the small talk and start strong as planned. The first minutes of the meeting should be noteworthy as you present your well-developed opening statements.

Your Opening Statement

> You: "Ms./Mr. (BLANK), thank you for your time today. I'm here to request (BLANK). I'm convinced the time has come for us to carefully consider committing organizational resources to the issue of (BLANK). Therefore, I've come prepared to answer your questions regarding this request."

With this straightforward statement, you're off and running.

1. You've clearly and specifically stated what you want.

2. You've clearly and specifically stated why you want it.

3. You've clearly and specifically stated your openness to questions.

It's game on. Questions must come. So don't be caught off guard if/ when questions come quickly. Be even less surprised when the first questions deal with project cost.

Decision-maker:

> "I'm interested in hearing more, but my first question is simple. How much will this cost?"

This question allows you to begin revealing the full scope of your preparatory efforts. You knew it was coming. No surprise there. But you should always remember to never—REPEAT NEVER—go into this meeting less than fully prepared for this question and the others that will predictably follow, knowing how to deliver the right answers when asked, all the while recognizing and avoiding the wrong ones.

Three Wrong Answers

Individuals who impetuously approach decision-makers with ideas, fueled by the passion and emotion of the moment but with little to no preparation, are virtually assured of unceremonious failure. As depicted earlier by the flowchart, to earn the right to move to a decision-maker's second question (then third, fourth, and fifth), an individual must first successfully answer the question immediately before him or her. An inability to do so is certain to earn even the most earnest "idea seller" an unceremonious "stop."

So once again we return to the first expected question: "How much will this cost?"

Fail to answer this first question "right" and your foray into the *Earning the Right to Be Heard* process is sure to be short-lived. Experience teaches that woefully unprepared individuals generally respond to this predictable question incorrectly. Too frequently they implemented an ill-advised "shoot from the hip" idea-selling strategy. With it, failure is usually immediate, but the negative repercussions associated with that failure last far longer.

There are at least three completely wrong answers to the "How much will this cost?" question. Wise presenters should be aware of all three to avoid falling victim to any of them.

Wrong Answer #1: "I don't know."
Wrong Answer #2: "Not much."
Wrong Answer #3: "It doesn't matter, we need it."

Let's consider each answer individually and why it would be viewed as wrong in the eyes of any conscientious decision-maker.

Question: "How much will this cost?"
Wrong Answer #1: "I don't know."

An answer of "I don't know" provides unmistakable proof that you've not done your homework. It gives an indication that you're expecting someone else to do the "legwork" for an initiative you're proposing and profess to believe in. Finally, the response says to decision-makers: "Frankly, I don't realize—or care—that I'm wasting your time right now."

You may not realize or care, but I assure you the decision-maker will. Such a callous approach to a meeting you requested is sure to magnify the decision-maker's frustration created by its worthlessness. Expect that decision-maker to move quickly—to end the meeting. As far as he/she is concerned, you had your opportunity. You blew it.

Question: How much will this cost?"
Wrong Answer #2: "Not much."

How can this possibly be a wrong answer? some will wonder. *Aren't all decision-makers ultimately responsible for saving and managing money wisely?*

Actually, decision-makers are ultimately responsible for making good decisions. "Good," of course, is measured against various objectives established by the organization a decision-maker represents. If a good decision accomplishes objectives AND saves money, that's doubly good!

To one degree or another, decision-makers will always be concerned about the overall cost of any project or initiative. That's why the cost question usually takes precedence. But be advised—questioning cost first does not necessarily equate to cost mattering most. Here's why: Most seasoned decision-makers have felt the sting of some decision gone bad. Many regrettable decisions can be traced back to basic cost considerations, but not always in the way one might expect.

One vendor or service provider may have sported a lower price tag than did others. Tempted by the tantalizing lure of lower price alone, unfortunate decisions were made, ultimately resulting in inferior materials, shabby workmanship, unkept promises, unmet schedules, and the like.

Such unpleasant memories linger long in the minds (and reputations) of otherwise conscientious decision-makers. The truth is, big numbers don't always frighten the best decision-makers—but small numbers might. If/when the cost question receives a "not much" response, it's easy (and common) for a scarred (and scared) decision-maker to interpret "not much" as meaning not "worth much." The interpretation/assumption equates cost to value. Such an assumption is not always correct. But it's hard to argue that it doesn't happen, even with experienced decision-makers.

The moral is, don't be afraid of presenting what might seem to you to be a significant cost, as long as the cost is "legitimately defensible." If the future benefits of the initiative are significant enough and can be legitimately defended, the expected benefits may easily overcome any initial sticker shock.

Question: **How much will this cost?"**
Wrong Answer #3: **"It doesn't matter; we need it."**

Wrong Answer #3 is particularly frustrating for most decision-makers. Of course cost matters! Everyone should know that. For a serious seller of ideas to answer a sensible question with such a nonsensical response is both foolish and reckless. Foolish because it almost certainly will frustrate, and possibly infuriate, decision-makers. Reckless because it's unnecessary and avoidable.

When an untrained, unprepared individual is asked key questions by decision-makers, that person must answer. However, without solid reasoning and factual support developed in advance of the meeting, responses such as Wrong Answer #3 are the result.

Fueled by the combustible mixture of passion and emotion, plus the immediate pressure to respond, the seller's response may stop the process in its tracks. With those six ill-advised words—"It doesn't matter, we need it!"—he/she is also snuffing out future opportunities to wield personal influence.

Most every organization has far more needs, desires, and initiatives than available resources to fund them. Therefore, the successful seller and his/her initiative must stand out (in a good way). The best way to gain entrance into the inner sanctum of organizational decision-making is to effectively prove (sell) the worthiness of every aspect of the initiative currently under consideration. Wrong answers to foundational questions won't get you there—nor will a lack of evidence used to support your "right" answers.

The Proof Is in the Preparation

Once a decision-maker asks, "How much will this cost?" idea sellers should be prepared to immediately offer "proof." No hesitation.

SELLER:

> "I expected you to be concerned about the cost of this initiative—and rightfully so. Therefore, I've taken the time to prepare this written cost estimate for your review."

With that simple, straightforward statement, a single sheet of paper is presented to the decision-maker. This written proof is nothing more than a document created by you, containing information intended to support and assist you in answering the decision-maker's questions.

The effectiveness of proofs is anchored in a very few basic considerations. First, proofs are most effective when NOT used as "information dumps." Effective sellers utilize the "less is more" philosophy. Less information, more impact. Never bury decision-makers in unnecessary data. Why provide more information than is expected, needed, or that can be easily absorbed? It predictably slows the process. Expecting decision-makers to dig through an avalanche of information is frustrating to them and counterproductive to our purposes. Highlighting and sharing select data, rather than every possible detail, is what decision-makers appreciate most.

Proofs, when organized thoughtfully, enable decision-makers to quickly evaluate details of proposed initiatives and the precepts on which they're based. These proofs should not attempt to answer every conceivable question. Each proof should provide enough information to keep the decision-maker engaged, while answering the expected questions and supporting the advancement of our influence and opportunities. If a decision-maker asks for more information, fine. Agree to provide it. But don't be surprised when your basic proofs are more than was expected and enough to inform the decision.

Again, when the decision-maker asks for cost information, just hand him/her the first proof sheet bearing the heading: "Estimated Cost Analysis." Enter the meeting with at least two copies of this cost analysis—one for the decision-maker and one for you. Your copy allows you to review the detailed information along with the decision-maker, making necessary notes regarding specific points of discussion or concern that may arise.

By the way, if you're successful—if the decision-maker's questions keep coming—this proof-sharing process will be repeated a total of four times during your in-person, approximately 30-minute presentation. Answer that first question satisfactorily and a second question (most likely benefits-related) is sure to follow.

Therefore, come to this first meeting prepared with transition statements and individual proofs for every anticipated question. As the second, third, and fourth questions surface, you'll be appropriately prepared. Simply repeat a derivative of your earlier *"I expected you to be concerned about _____, so I've prepared this written _____ for your review"* statement. Deliver the statement, then share the corresponding proof sheet. Again, it's advisable to keep an extra copy of each proof handy for your personal review and note-taking.

Here's how the process should flow regarding the first four anticipated questions:

The COST Question

Step 1: DECISION-MAKER'S QUESTION:

> "How much will this cost?"

Step 2: YOUR TRANSITION STATEMENT:

> "I expected you to be concerned about the cost of this initiative—and rightly so. Therefore, I've taken the time to prepare this written cost estimate for your review."

Step 3: PROVIDE ONE-PAGE PROOF:

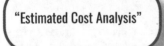

> "Estimated Cost Analysis"

Step 4: DISCUSSION FOLLOWS

Step 5: DECISION-MAKER ASKS NEXT QUESTION

The BENEFIT Question

Step 1: DECISION-MAKER'S QUESTION:

> "What benefits can be expected?"

Step 2: YOUR TRANSITION STATEMENT:

> "The available benefits this initiative can provide are considerable. I've created this list highlighting possible benefits for your review."

Step 3: PROVIDE ONE-PAGE PROOF:

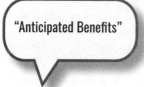

> "Anticipated Benefits"

Step 4: DISCUSSION FOLLOWS

Step 5: DECISION-MAKER ASKS NEXT QUESTION

The TIME Question

Step 1: DECISION-MAKER'S QUESTION:

"How much time will this require?"

Step 2: YOUR TRANSITION STATEMENT:

"In order to best use the time available,
I've created this timeline for your review."

Step 3: PROVIDE ONE-PAGE PROOF:

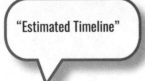

"Estimated Timeline"

Step 4: DISCUSSION FOLLOWS

Step 5: DECISION-MAKER ASKS NEXT QUESTION

The IMPLEMENTATION Question

Step 1: DECISION-MAKER'S QUESTION:

"How difficult will this project be to implement?"

Step 2: YOUR TRANSITION STATEMENT:

"Implementation will require coordination of several moving pieces. Here's a possible implementation plan to consider."

Step 3: PROVIDE ONE-PAGE PROOF:

"Suggested Implementation Plan"

Step 4: DISCUSSION FOLLOWS

Step 5: DECISION-MAKER ASKS NEXT QUESTION

Providing written, one-page proofs supporting your answers to each of the four questions offers evidence of your thoughtfulness and preparation. The proofs will allow the decision-maker's focus to be directed and maintained.

Notice there is no requirement for a proof for the fifth anticipated ("CONSEQUENCE") question. This is not an accidental omission. The reason will become clear during our "consequence" discussion in chapter 13.

Taking Care of the Little Things

There's one other important point to consider before leaving this section. It may seem insignificant, but I assure you this little thing can have a big effect on the outcome of the *Earning the Right to Be Heard* process.

Many people rightfully strive to be environmentally conscious in all their activities. Good for you, and because of you, good for all of us. However, in this one instance I feel compelled to sound a cautionary note. You may have thought it wasteful to use an individual sheet of paper for each question's written proof. It might be tempting to disregard my recommended use of multiple individual sheets in favor of compiling information onto one or two sheets total. Don't do it. Here's why.

Each step of the *Earning the Right to Be Heard* process has been carefully evaluated for its respective value—right down to the use of individual sheets of paper. Decision-makers are initially surprised, then observably pleased, when an initiative presenter (you) produces that first sheet, the proof, containing supporting documentation.

By the time the second (benefit) question is asked and that second related proof is offered, some decision-makers become almost giddy with delight and anticipation. This unexpected trove of written information dovetails nicely with the "logic and rationale" approach that professional decision-makers prefer.

The chances of getting what we want (our secondary objective) and *Earning the Right to Be Heard* (our primary objective) improve as we're asked, then answer correctly, each of the decision-maker's questions. Unfortunately, if you were to provide all the information on a single sheet of paper, then he/she could (would) read ahead. Your ability to control the release of information, the narrative, and the discussion would be unalterably diminished.

Direct and Indirect Costs

For the "cost" proof, what should be included?

Our basic "cost" proof should include a minimum of two categories: direct AND indirect costs. Estimating an initiative's direct costs is fairly obvious, elementary, and necessary. No self-respecting decision-maker would expect—or accept—less.

But by including practical indirect costs, many decision-makers' expectations are exceeded. Why? Simply put, many individuals have learned to withhold from decision-making discussions costs that are not readily obvious. Consider them "hidden costs."

If hidden costs are not obvious, why muddy the decision-making waters by including them? some might question.

Here's why. Most experienced decision-makers have learned to expect that certain costs and expenditures have been, are being, or will be hidden from them. They also know that such information is eventually revealed via the need for amended budgets, project overrun reporting, or missed delivery deadlines—each having real cost and time consequences. It's no wonder decision-makers have become cautious (suspicious) about the "true" cost of projects.

Therefore, when a team member—you—voluntarily shines a light on indirect project costs, decision-makers are sure to sit up and take note. While others may question the wisdom of possibly derailing your suggested initiative by adding "unnecessary" cost projections to the initiative's proposal, decision-makers won't. They generally view such a step as the equivalent of laying of a cornerstone of trust. The gesture serves as a goodwill marker in the expanding relationship between you and the decision-maker. When relationships expand, personal influence expands with it and additional opportunities materialize. Consider the following working example.

Brenda's Opening Statement:

"Mr. Malek, thanks for your time today. I'm here to request the purchase of a new copier for the marketing, sales, and service departments. It's time to upgrade the copier for use throughout our combined departments. I've come prepared to answer your questions regarding this request."

Mr. Malek's 1st Question:

"Brenda, okay. How much does the copier you're recommending cost?"

Brenda's Transitional Statement:

"I've prepared this written cost estimate for your review (shares "Estimated Cost Analysis" proof). I'll give you a minute to look it over."

The "Cost" Proof

SUNDIAL COPIER ESTIMATED COST ANALYSIS
(Fictional Example)

Recommended Copier:

Sundial HVP LaserPro 1957 P-Series

Capabilities Required:

Color print/copy/scan
Multiple remote e-print users (digitally managed documents)
Security authentication
Advanced finishing (staple, sew, and pamphlet printing)
High speed (25 pages printed per minute)
Multiple users (25 total)

Direct Costs:

Purchase price $12,750.00
Tax (@6.5%) 812.50
Delivery & setup 500.00
3-year "no-fault" warranty 4,500.00
Total direct costs $18,562.50

Indirect Costs:

Total cost of user training
(25 users @ $25/hour
average wage, 2.5 hours
of user training) $ 1,562.50
Total Project Cost: $20,125.00

Never Pad

On the heels of presenting the numbers above, there is a brief but important word to the wise to be offered. When developing and communicating the "Estimated Cost Analysis" for any project you're preparing to pitch, NEVER PAD THE NUMBERS! It may be tempting to add a financial buffer here or there, but you can't afford to succumb to this temptation. It's just not worth it.

If a decision-maker discovers you've intentionally manipulated or "doctored" the numbers (costs) on any proposal, for any reason, in any way, your influence problems are just beginning. It's fair to assume your chances of ultimately getting what you want or *Earning the Right to Be Heard*—now or ever—will be greatly and immediately diminished. Again I say, it's just not worth it.

Stand Firm

Once the cost proof has been shared, expect discussion to follow. Questions may come fast and furiously or slow and deliberately. Expect either, then simply adapt your pace of response to that of the decision-maker. But never rush. There's no prize awaiting the fastest finisher. Allow the decision-maker time to consider and become comfortable with the information being shared, the implications, and the process you're leading.

That's an important point. Remember, it was you who requested this meeting; therefore, you're responsible for leading it—gently, but professionally. Keep in mind that this is probably new territory for your decision-maker, too. It's usually him or her at the helm of such a meeting.

Therefore, initially, this "role reversal" may be confusing. A bit of subtle coaching may be needed. That, too, is your responsibility. Own it.

For example, it's quite possible (even probable) that in reviewing your cost proof, the decision-maker will spontaneously ask a question (albeit prematurely) from one of the other four predictable question categories (benefit, time, implementation, or consequence). Such a diversion might begin with a comment/question such as:

Mr. Malek:

"These cost estimates are intriguing, but I can't help but wonder if you have taken into consideration the possible confusion of three different departments, plus remote workers, all depending on the same copier?"

It's a great question—legitimate, on point, and worthy of a direct answer. In fact, you've already anticipated such a question and have prepared to address it directly, albeit later in the presentation. You could respond to it now. But for the sake of the overall process, it would be better to save it for the "implementation" question discussion, if possible.

What do you do? How might you delicately guide the decision-maker back to where you'd like him/her to be at this point in the process? It's really quite simple. If/when such a temporary deflection does occur, politely offer:

Brenda:

"Mr. Malek, I'm happy to address that question. I'm prepared to do so. But first, I want to be sure I've answered all your cost-related questions. Have we missed anything, or are you ready to move on?"

Simple, polite, professional, confident, well-planned, and well-executed. All expertly controlled by you. You're encouraged to keep this particular response readily available. This example is a go-to option whenever any question pops up that you would prefer to address later.

By the way, this response is NOT an attempt to dodge the question. It IS an attempt to reorder it, if possible, in the interest of fostering a seamless process. As a rule, the decision-maker will be agreeable to following your lead as long as he/she is assured the question will eventually be addressed.

By the way, you will instinctively know it's time to move on to the next aspect of the proposal when the decision-maker signals his acceptance of and comfort with the handling of the question before him/her. In such a circumstance, you may expect a comment like this:

Mr. Malek:

"The detail contained in this document helps me understand the estimated costs for the overall project. But I still need to know what benefits can be expected."

Notice the difference? The decision-maker is not randomly leapfrogging from one category to another. Brenda has created and is managing a process flow in which, once comfort with one category (in this case, cost) has been established, it's natural to move to the next category (benefits). That's the way the process is designed to work.

Batting .500 Is Not the Objective

Never get your hopes up. You shouldn't expect a decision-maker to approve any request after discussing just the cost-related questions. Cost is one factor—an *important* factor—but certainly not the *only* determining factor. Discerning decision-makers will want more information before they are comfortable making any final decision.

If, on some exceptionally rare occasion, a decision-maker does disrupt the natural order of things by moving to approve your request directly after the cost discussion, be assured that the decision had been made earlier—before your conversation even began. The actual reason or motivation for such quick, decisive action may never be fully known. For our purposes, we'll just call it "fortunate timing." But realize the "yes" in this case was not the result of your pitch.

You may argue, "So, what's wrong with that? I got what I wanted, didn't I?"

Yes, you did. Or at least a part of what you wanted. Remember, there have been two objectives identified from the beginning. Getting what you wanted was one—the secondary objective. But once the quick approval came, your opportunity to nail down the primary objective— *Earning the Right to Be Heard*—was lost. Not necessarily lost forever, but certainly lost for the moment. The preferred goal, regardless of the final decision, would have been to lead the decision-maker through the entire process so that he/she could better understand both the request and the value of your individual effort.

Remember our flowchart? The rectangular symbol marked "predetermined process step" (the COST question) requires a decision be made before any further action/movement can be taken. If the question is not answered to the decision-maker's level of satisfaction, the process stops right there. It will remain paused until the decision-maker's questions/ concerns are satisfactorily resolved.

On the other hand, if/when you are successful in answering the decision-maker's initial question, the process can move forward to the next "predetermined process step" (the BENEFIT question), and so on.

The goal, of course, is to keep the process moving steadily toward the successful completion of our dual objectives.

A Concise Review

Always remember to never—REPEAT NEVER—go into the first meeting with the decision-maker less than fully prepared with answers to each of the anticipated "five questions."

Big numbers don't always frighten good decision-makers—but small numbers might. Subconsciously, cost is often equated with value.

If future benefits of this initiative (or any other) are significant enough, the benefits alone may easily overcome any initial sticker shock.

Proofs—or written documents supporting your answers to the five key process questions—should be designed with the "less is more" concept in mind, which is why it is advisable to create separate proofs for each question. Don't bury decision-makers in data; instead, give them the resources they need to follow your lead and pique their interest about what's to come.

Never expect a decision-maker to approve a request after discussing just the cost question. Discerning decision-makers will want to learn more, unless they have already rendered a decision on the subject in advance.

CHAPTER 10

WHAT ARE THE BENEFITS?

How Much Is Too Much?

Whenever an average individual considers the cost of almost anything, an expected first inclination is to compare that cost against something similar with which they are familiar. For example, when refueling on a road trip, it's only natural to compare the cost of fuel to fuel purchased elsewhere on the journey. When stopping for a meal, one instinctively compares menu prices against prices paid at another eatery. When arriving at a destination, one compares room rates against prices at other lodging stops along the route.

For the sake of argument, let's assume for each of these situations (fuel, food, and lodging) that the prices being paid are higher than previously experienced for comparable goods and services. Under such conditions, two important questions arise:

- How much is too much?

- Is it worth it?

How much is too much? Well, that's tricky. It depends. It's certainly "too much" if one lacks the resources (or access to resources) necessary to pay for the purchase. Practically speaking, that's when we learn the valuable life lesson of "doing without."

But something might also be considered "too much" when the ability to pay IS present (having the resources or access to them) but the purchase decision requires a significant sacrifice of something else of value to the decision-maker (money, time, credibility, influence, etc.). It's then that the significance of the sacrifice must be evaluated alongside the anticipated benefits.

For the sacrifice to be made voluntarily, benefits to be gained by the choice must be determined to be of greater, longer-lasting value, worth, or usefulness than that which is to be sacrificed. For most of us, that's an exceptionally difficult determination to make, especially in real time with the pressure on. When decisions are that difficult personally, most nonprofessional decision-makers would simply determine "that's too much."

However, the professional decision-makers are called upon and expected to make such difficult determinations regularly. Not necessarily about food, fuel, and lodging, but about issues that would benefit the organizations they represent. They must look deeper into every opportunity, measuring necessary sacrifices against all possible benefits. Sometimes cost proves to be the deciding factor. Sometimes not.

So, when is it worth it? That's an even tricker determination decision-makers must make. For our purposes here, let's consider two definitions from a simple Web search related to the word "worth."

> **"Worth" defined (adjective):**
> sufficiently good, important, or interesting to justify a specified action
>
> **"Worth" defined (noun):**
> the value equivalent to that of someone or something under consideration

To explore these definitions further, consider this example. The following situation finds two friends discussing recent experiences with their respective tax accountants. Read on:

Friend 1: *"I just filed my annual income tax returns. My accountant charged me $300 for his services."*

Friend 2: *"Yeah, I just filed mine, too, but my accountant charged me $1,500."*

Friend 1: *"FIFTEEN HUNDRED DOLLARS! You've gotta be kidding! I would NEVER, EVER pay $1,500 to have my taxes done!"*

Friend 2: *"I wouldn't either if it wasn't worth it to me. But my new accountant prepared a comprehensive report listing a number of legitimate deductions and tax-saving strategies that my previous accountant had routinely overlooked. This year alone I'm due a refund of just over $4,500."*

Friend 1: (pauses, thinking) *"What's your accountant's name again?"*

The worthiness outlined in this example can be considered twofold. First, the initial worth identified by Friend 1 is directly associated with realizing a small tax bill (*sufficiently good, important, or interesting to justify a specified action*). But there's an equally important example of worth acknowledged by Friend 2.

Friend 2 could appreciate Friend 1's considerable low bill. But he also recognized the worthy contribution an individual (Friend 2's new accountant) can make (*the value equivalent to that of someone or something under consideration*). In the end, worth was determined to be available for both friends.

That represents the very essence of this influence-building process. As stressed again and again, our secondary objective here is to deliver appropriate information to decision-makers in such a way as to sufficiently make a "specified action" (our proposal) "justifiable." But the primary objective of *Earning the Right to Be Heard* always remains the same. The "value equivalent" in the way you present your proposals should be so blatantly obvious that decision-makers can't consider the worth of the "something" (the initiative) without also considering the even greater worth of the "someone" (the seller of the initiative)—you!

The Most Important Question

As the seller of the initiative, you've already made significant progress. Having been asked the decision-maker's first question, you met the challenge at hand with a well-developed, effective response. How do I know for sure you answered the COST question satisfactorily? I know because you've now been asked Question 2 ("What benefits can be expected?"). That's exactly the progress we're working and preparing for.

You must now turn your attention to dealing with this second question. Make no mistake, this is the MOST important question. That's right, the BENEFIT question is actually the most important of all the five questions to be anticipated. Why? Because the BENEFIT question is the basis for clarifying and determining the value equivalent—the worth—of virtually every decision to be made going forward.

"So, Phil, you're saying the primary determining factor as to whether or not my initiative gets approved is not what it will cost, but rather the value of the benefits it provides?"

In essence, yes. It's never my intent to downplay the importance of an initiative's cost or any of the other questions expected along the way. All are important. All must be given serious consideration. All must be appropriately prepared for and responded to.

But experience has taught me the intrinsic worth of highlighting multifaceted benefits. Said a different way, if something is proven to be valuable enough, the majority of the time decision-makers will find a way to justify the cost. Therefore, decisions are directly related to the benefits. It's your job to capture and communicate those benefits and the too-often overlooked value (worth) they represent.

What Benefits Can Be Expected?

Your thoughtful creation, preparation, and presentation of the first proof ("Estimated Cost Analysis") to answer Question #1 earned you the right to be asked Question #2. Now your job is to repeat the process carefully in order to answer the BENEFIT question. This section will help you identify and effectively communicate the benefits of your initiative.

There should be no question, confusion, or hesitation when the right time arrives to unveil your second proof. The opportunity is right when the decision-maker says something like this:

Mr. Malek's 2nd Question:

"Brenda, the estimated cost analysis was helpful. Thank you. But let's face facts. Twenty thousand dollars is a lot of money. I'm wondering how the purchase of this copier can generate enough benefit to justify the cost?"

Brenda's Transitional Statement:

"It is a considerable amount of money. That's why I spent so much time analyzing the overall benefits. Look at my list of plausible benefits related to this request."

The "Benefits" Proof

SUNDIAL COPIER ANTICIPATED BENEFITS
(Fictional Example)

Economic Benefits to Be Considered:

1. Reduced copier downtime
2. Reduced "user" wait time
3. Reduced maintenance/repair costs
4. Extended "life expectancy" of hardware
5. Free software updates
6. Guaranteed 5-year "no question trade-in or buy back" option

Organizational Benefits to Be Considered:

1. User security authentication (for access to confidential documents)
2. Digital data file storage (for repetitious print requirements)
3. Digital document management (advanced "save, share, and print" options)
4. Remote access (available to employees traveling or working remotely)
5. State-of-the-line data imaging
6. Controlled access to confidential information (new product development, pricing)

Efficiency Benefits to Be Considered:

1. Significant productivity increases (22 printed pages per minute)
2. Advanced touchscreen technology
3. High-quality custom printing (proposals, annual reports, marketing materials)
4. Faster turnaround (marketing pieces, proposals, engineering change documents)

Environmental Benefits to Be Considered:

1. "Energy Saver" enhanced technology
   (environmentally friendly)
2. Reduced toner usage
   (25% reduction expected as compared to current usage)
3. Reusable toner cartridges (environmentally friendly)

The Plausibility Factor

The number of potential benefits that could be included in this (or any) "Anticipated Benefits" proof is essentially infinite. There is no "right" number and no established limit. The only real limits to creating such a list involve your own limited investigation and imagination. This fictional example just offered is intended as a model for consideration.

The various benefits categories (economic, organizational, efficiency, and environmental) included in the sample worksheet represent categories of my own choosing. These specific categories should not be thought of as the only categories available or ones that must be utilized in every future proposal.

When proposing different initiatives, additional, possibly different, benefit categories may be better suited for inclusion than the ones used here. Additional categories might also include (in no particular order): safety benefits; competitive benefits; growth benefits; marketing benefits; time benefits; and social, civic, and/or community benefits.

Just as these categories can be expanded, so can the individual benefits listed within the categories. The category list you create should be completely yours and completely aligned with the particular initiative you are proposing. Again, own it.

Although the categories may be changed at will, one point must remain constant: all benefits listed must always be plausible. If they're not, don't include them. Period. For the idea presenter (you) to be taken seriously by decision-makers, the benefits presented must first be taken seriously by decision-makers. To be taken seriously, any and all benefits included must be plausible/reasonable. In this case, you will not be known by the friends you keep but rather by the benefits you promote.

None of us has access to crystal balls by which we can predict an unfailing future. It's futile to try to envision each and every scenario that might eventually befall future enacted initiatives. Every logical person, particularly decision-makers, understands that. It's foolishness to think otherwise.

It's equally illogical, ill-advised, and foolish to make promises of any kind to decision-makers simply to "sell" your ideas. Especially problematic are promises indicating certain benefits will undoubtedly be realized with the approval of your initiative.

Experienced, pragmatic decision-makers know better. They know such claims or guarantees can't be supported. Therefore, in the eyes of decision-makers, those who foolishly make such claims unwittingly damage their own chances for legitimacy, trust, and the possibility of *Earning the Right to Be Heard*. Overpromising and under-delivering is not the recommended way to be known/remembered. Your goal is to build personal influence, not destroy it.

In light of such considerations, the "plausibility factor" becomes critically important. Again, "plausible" benefits are not guaranteed benefits and should never be presented as such. Plausible benefits, instead, are benefits that, when presented and explained in proper context, seem "reasonable or probable" and, therefore, merit further consideration.

As you identify and consider individual benefits to be included in your future "Anticipated Benefits" proofs, your goal must always to be ensure that each benefit listed passes the plausibility test.

Legitimately Defensible

Contained in the "Anticipated Benefits" illustration a few pages back are a total of 19 unique benefits. For the overall purposes of *Earning the Right to Be Heard*, there's nothing magical about the number 19. An acceptable number of benefits could just as easily be 9 or 39. The actual number is basically immaterial. Far more important is the legitimate defensibility of each benefit listed.

As referenced earlier, decision-makers can be a suspicious lot. That's not intended to be an insult. On the contrary, it is intended to make idea sellers aware that additional proof may be necessary for cost estimates and anticipated benefits. Remember, with each decision a decision-maker makes, his/her reputation hangs in the balance. Therefore, decision-makers are justified in being cautiously suspicious in order to ensure the information on which they base their decisions is solid.

To that end, once the "Anticipated Benefits" proof is in the hands of the decision-maker, certain reactions can be expected. Don't be surprised when a decision-maker peruses the list and initiates a deeper dive into specific components of the proof.

As the decision-maker begins to ask questions, there are a few important points to keep in mind.

1) Don't expect the review of benefits to be linear.

Decision-makers are prone to question those benefits that "jump off the page" at them. Don't expect a particular rhyme or reason to the order. Questions may come from the top of the list, then move downward. Or from the bottom upward. Or, of course, decision-makers' questions may jump around indiscriminately. There's no right or wrong approach here.

Just remember, flexibility is key. Stay loose and be prepared to respond to questions however they might come.

2) Obvious benefits may not be questioned.

Not every benefit listed will invite individual scrutiny. The ones you believe are most valuable (or significant) may actually receive the silent treatment—no questions asked. Don't despair. It doesn't mean the decision-maker has a problem with the benefit or is frustrated in some way. On the contrary, the most obvious benefits are often ignored because they are just that—*obvious* benefits. Decision-makers are trained to recognize the obvious quickly, focusing instead on that which is less obvious. They will dig deeper into the benefits that require more information or explanation.

3) A request for more information does not necessarily indicate a problem.

When the decision-maker asks for more information regarding any particular benefit listed—and you should expect him/her to do so—be prepared to share specific additional data. Let's look at how this plays out in our continuing example:

Mr. Malek:

"Brenda, can you explain more about benefit number three, the "reduced maintenance/repair costs" item?

Brenda:

"Yes, sir. I checked with Admin regarding the past three years' maintenance costs for our existing copier. We've averaged just under $1,100 per year in repairs—direct costs. Of course, that doesn't include the indirect costs created during downtime while awaiting repair."

4) Remember, brevity is your friend.

When a decision-maker asks a question, he/she is not asking for a 10-minute dissertation or for the answer to spin into other unrelated areas not being questioned. Again, decision makers don't appreciate "information dumps," be they written or verbal. A brief, on-point response to a specific question is always welcome. It is certain to engender more respect than a long-winded, rambling response ever could.

5) Don't fake it.

If asked a BENEFIT question and you know the answer, give it. Directly. Confidently. Without pause or hesitation. But if asked a BENEFIT question and you don't know the answer, NEVER pretend you do. Trying to talk your way out of or around some difficulty usually means you just create more difficulty for yourself.

A wiser approach is never to include a questionable benefit on your list in the first place. Why set yourself up for failure unnecessarily? When the practical value of even one benefit is questionable, all the benefits may suddenly become so in the eyes of decision-makers. That's a surefire way to "stop" the forward progress as depicted by our flowchart example.

Don't try to bluff your way through. Do your homework and be prepared to defend each and every benefit, whether asked to do so or not.

To legitimately defend the value of each point of your presentation to decision-makers means you've taken full responsibility. To do it well leads decision-makers to be even more impressed. When decision-makers are impressed, expect them to ask more questions.

In the Spirit of Full Disclosure

There's one final thought to be considered before shifting attention away from the BENEFIT question to the TIME question (Question #3) to follow. As emphasized previously, identifying all plausible benefits is critically important to establishing the value of any initiative. Equally important is establishing and maintaining the trustworthiness of the initiative seller (you) in the eyes of the initiative buyer (the decision-maker).

To build and sustain a rock-solid trust factor, you should voluntarily identify any known risks associated with your recommended initiative, along with appropriate actions to follow. It's easy enough to say, "I have full confidence in the initiative I'm proposing today and the benefits associated with it. However, in the spirit of full disclosure, there are a couple of unknowns you should be aware of." Then voluntarily mention (before being asked) what those unknowns are, your practical concerns, and the basic actions necessary to mitigate those same concerns.

Identifying risks associated with your proposals, as counterintuitive as it may initially seem, is almost always a positive step forward in the *Earning the Right to Be Heard* process. Don't hesitate to plan for and take that step as may be necessary.

A Concise Review

The BENEFIT question is the basis for clarifying and determining the value of virtually every decision to be made.

If something is shown to be valuable enough, decision-makers will usually find a way to justify the cost.

Overpromising and under-delivering is not the way to be known/remembered. Your goal is to build personal influence, not destroy it.

When relevant, disclose potential risks or unknowns associated with your proposal. Doing so will enhance your credibility and boost your influence.

CHAPTER 11

HOW MUCH TIME WILL IT TAKE?

Simple as 1–2–3

Can anything really be as simple as 1–2–3? Maybe. Consider this simplified analysis of the *Earning the Right to Be Heard* process as outlined so far:

Step 1: Idea/initiative identified, developed, and introduced to decision-maker(s).

Step 2: Primary questions (COST, BENEFIT) prepared for, in advance.

Step 3: Secondary questions (TIME, IMPLEMENTATION, CONSEQUENCE) prepared for, in advance.

Basically, that's it—simple as 1–2–3. So, don't be surprised when this process begins to feel more comfortable. You're making steady progress toward a predictable and desirable outcome.

Upon successfully answering the primary COST and BENEFIT questions, a minimum of three more predictable questions can be expected to follow. Because they are consistently asked under similar circumstances, they, too, should be prepared for in advance of the initial meeting.

Therefore, again, it's as simple as 1–2–3.

1. Understand and trust the process.

2. Anticipate questions and prepare comprehensive responses in advance.

3. Deliver the prepared responses/information with confidence.

When Can You Start?

Whenever decision-makers have their most pressing questions answered (COST and BENEFIT), most will turn their attention to pressing second-tier considerations, of which TIME is almost always key. As a corporate human resources manager, whenever I pursued a new recruit to fill an open position, it was critical that I learned at least three things up front. To do less would have been a colossal waste of time.

1. Was the recruit interested in working with us?

2. Was his/her salary expectation in line with what we could afford?

3. Would hiring him/her provide discernible benefits for the organization?

If the answers to these primary questions were unqualified "yeses," you could be sure it wouldn't be long before I asked a fourth question: "When can you start?"

As it relates to selling your ideas utilizing the *Earning the Right to Be Heard* process, cost and benefits may be considered the highest hurdles to be overcome. Once you've successfully surpassed them, it does not mean you're home free—yet. Neither does it mean your two original objectives have been realized—yet. What it does mean is that tremendous progress is being made. In that vein, as both seller and buyer sense progress being made and momentum building, soon both can be expected to turn their focus to how long it might be before the full range of benefits can be realized.

How Much Time Will It Take?

Mr. Malek's 3rd Question:

"Brenda, I appreciate the opportunity to work through the 'Anticipated Benefits' proof. You've got me wondering. If I was to approve this copier request, how long would it take before the copier was in place and functional?"

Brenda's Transitional Statement:

"Mr. Malek, take a look at this. With your approval of this request today, this is the 'Estimated Timeline' for successfully completing all stages of this project.

The "Time" Proof

SUNDIAL COPIER ESTIMATED TIMELINE
(Fictional Example)

Stage 1: Receive Approval

- Approval received (today) February 22, 20—
- Confirm purchase specifications (with Purchasing) February 26, 20—
- Secure purchase order February 26, 20—

Stage 2: Order, Shipping, Delivery, Setup

- Place order for copier with local dealer February 28, 20—
- Copier expected (no later than) March 15, 20—
- Coper delivered and set up March 17, 20—

Stage 3: User Training (25 users @ 2.5 hours training per user)

- Session 1 (8 users/1:00–3:30 pm) March 20, 20—
- Session 2 (8 users/9:00–11:30 am) March 21, 20—
- Session 3 (9 users/1:00–3:30 pm) March 22, 20—
- Make-up session (9:00–11:30 am) March 25, 20—

Stage 4: Copier Available for Full Utilization

- Delivery, setup, and training complete/fully functional March 26, 20—

Time Is Money

Virtually every organizational decision-maker possessing the equivalent of a week's worth of decision-making experience can be expected to understand the special relationship between time and money. Therefore, if you wish to influence such decision-makers in the future, it's advisable that you become keenly aware of it, too. That, and how to use that time-money connection to your advantage.

Here's another given. Regardless of how good (or mediocre) your initiative presentation may end up being, the decision-maker simply WILL NOT approve your request on the day of its presentation. Sorry, it's not going to happen. It could happen the next day, the next week, the next month, or, of course, possibly not at all. But you should know it won't happen on the same day it's being introduced.

Why not? Explained simply, that's not how decision-makers are trained to respond. Decision-makers pride themselves on being contemplative and deliberate in processing information before finalizing their decision. As badly as you might want (and push for) a speedy decision and quick action, in the eyes of a professional decision-maker, hasty actions are not conducive to solid decision-making. Contemplation and deliberation take time. Some things just can't be rushed.

Why then, you might wonder, *did you suggest in the transitional statement example that a decision might be made today? After all, didn't Brenda imply that such a possibility existed when she said to Mr. Malek, "With your approval of this request today..."? Why suggest something could happen when you're sure it won't?*

If that's what you're thinking, good catch. There's a good reason that phrase is included. It's purely psychological.

Here's a fact: Every decision-maker worth his or her salt has been trained to accept the age-old "time is money" mantra. Therefore, if the decision-maker is already convinced that the benefits of this initiative outweigh the costs, we'd like a public commitment to that effect. Until such a commitment is made, action can't be taken.

But remember, decision-makers are by nature contemplative and deliberate. They are not prone to deciding and acting quickly or rashly. So your best option for speeding this process along is to subtly remind the decision-maker that lost time equates to lost money. The psychological conundrum equating delay and deliberation with lost money (or opportunity) can be a powerful catalyst for some truly committed decision-makers.

It's not necessarily a bad thing if decision-makers think to themselves, *Even though I'm hesitant to rush this decision, it's possible that I'll miss more benefits if I don't move quickly.* It doesn't always work out that way. But occasionally, you might hear these words a bit sooner than you might have otherwise:

Mr. Malek:

"Brenda, I've thought this initiative through. I can't see any reason why we shouldn't move forward on this project. I suggest you go ahead and get the process underway."

Unidentified Needs and Expectations

Another technique exists for establishing more decision-maker buy-in and therefore should be considered. During the initial portion of your presentation, decision-makers were encouraged to participate actively by asking questions. Once the question(s) had been posed, you responded with your prepared response (proofs). With the TIME question, it's helpful to intentionally change the flow of the narrative slightly.

Once you've delivered your "Estimated Timeline" for the decision-maker's review and consideration, consider preemptively asking the following question of your own:

Brenda's Question:

> "Mr. Malek, as I created this 'Estimated Timeline' I tried to anticipate timing conflicts this initiative might have with general business operations. But I'm afraid I might have missed something. Is there anything you're aware of that I need to build into the timeline for greater accuracy or efficiency?"

This is a really solid question from at least three different perspectives. First, it's solid in that it allows, even invites, outside involvement and input. Such a voluntary invitation by the idea initiator gives credible evidence of willingness and commitment to make the initiative the best it can be, regardless of who's involved or who might get the credit.

Secondly, the question offers solid indication of your awareness of and interest in the organization as a whole and not just your little slice of it. Influence and opportunities are not always found in or confined to your little corner of the world. In various ways, it's wise to expand your awareness and availability—your scope and reach. Taking time to consider your initiative's impact (if at all) on the bigger, broader workforce and workplace environment can be a real positive for progressive-minded sellers and buyers alike.

Finally, it's almost always a great idea to allow someone (including decision-makers) some measure of engagement with and personal ownership of general ideas and initiatives. Personal ownership almost always translates into heightened levels of support for the initiative and the presenter—support that can be expected to continue past the decision-making stage, well into the implementation stage. A good rule of thumb to remember as it relates to personal influence enhancement is this: *people tend to support and promote that which they have helped to create and develop.*

Be sure to ask the decision-maker if there is any reason for alterations to be made to the currently established timeline itself. It's always better to adapt a timeline at this stage than to have the process delayed later on because of some unforeseen, unanticipated timing glitch.

Always Pad

You may recall back in chapter 9, the "cost" chapter, that there was a brief section entitled "Never Pad." In it, the point was emphatically made that although tempting to do so, it's never wise to add a "buffer" (unwarranted

People tend to support and promote that which they have helped to create and develop.

dollars) to any project estimate. The numbers quoted need to stand (or fall) on their own. Otherwise, not only is your initiative in jeopardy, but your personal influence is as well.

Yes, we all know budget "buffering" or "padding" happens. Some individuals pride themselves on their supposed mastery of various clandestine budgeting shenanigans, intentionally adding in more to one budget category than necessary in hopes of covering a feared or anticipated reduction in some other area.

For some, it's little more than a game, the primary objective of which is just to get what they want. You, on the other hand, are playing a completely different game. Your primary objective is an unshakeable personal commitment to *Earning the Right to Be Heard*, as you strive to advance your influence, not lessen it.

Admittedly, getting what we want is nice. Immediate gratification generally is. But getting what we want is our secondary objective. Our primary objective is to build sustained trust and influence over time. Therefore, the original point was driven home rather emphatically: NEVER PAD THE NUMBERS!

But that was chapter 9, whose focus was on cost considerations. This is chapter 11, and the new focus is directed to time considerations. Your primary and secondary objectives remain the same. Nothing has changed there. So it may be a bit surprising to read the following words while in the process of developing and communicating the "Estimated Timeline." The new advice is—ALWAYS PAD THE NUMBERS!

Why the change of heart?

As it relates to money, the numbers tend to speak for themselves. There is either enough, not enough, or just the right amount. Relatively speaking, financial numbers are not that hard to determine.

The effect of time, on the other hand, is governed by a number of key (often unseen) variables. Despite your best efforts, these variables often remain outside your control.

For example, the most obvious variable is the decision-maker. Try as you might, you have no real control regarding when (even if) a decision-maker will approve the project you're promoting. But for the sake of argument, let's assume the decision-maker approves your request in a timely manner. Additional time challenges are still a distinct possibility.

With the decision-maker's approval in hand, there remains the issue of getting the necessary supporting documentation from Purchasing (or other administrative personnel). The required PO (purchase order), which seemed like a no-brainer when you were developing the timeline, ends up being a nightmare.

You learn Brett, the purchasing clerk, is out through the end of the week with a case of the flu. Daphne, the purchasing manager, is enjoying the last few days of her honeymoon in Tahiti. No one else is authorized (or knows how) to release a PO. So while Brett is bedridden nursing a fever and Daphne is poolside nursing a tropical drink, your PO languishes, gathering dust in an inbox for want of a single signature. That's three unplanned days added to your timeline.

Upon Daphne's return, the PO is quickly signed and executed. It's immediately forwarded to the local copier dealer, where the official order for the new Sundial HVP LaserPro 1957 P-Series copier is finally placed. The salesperson is excited.

Three hours later, you get an unsolicited call from that same salesperson. He's not so excited now. He just talked with the manufacturer. There's been a work stoppage at their manufacturing plant on the West Coast—some unresolved labor issue. Delivery trucks will be idled for the

EARNING THE RIGHT TO BE HEARD

next several days. The salesperson promised to call with an update once the issue gets resolved.

I could continue this worst-case example. I won't. You get the picture. Things happen—things that are totally unexpected and completely out of your control.

Nevertheless, your "Estimated Timeline" indicated the project would be completed and the copier up and running within one month. You're still fine. Why? Because you padded the numbers.

In a perfect situation, you estimated the project would take 15 days to be completed. But thankfully, you didn't create your "Estimated Timeline" as such. Realizing perfect situations are modern-day fairytales, you intentionally built two more weeks into the estimate on the front end. Therefore, you're still fine. No harm, no foul. If you can finish the project ahead of schedule, you're a superhero. Finish right on time and you're still a hero. Remember, when it comes to time, the time is always right to pad those numbers.

A Concise Review

If you wish to influence decision-makers, you should become keenly aware of their understanding of the relationship between time and money and how to use that knowledge to your advantage.

Regardless of how good your initiative presentation may end up being, the decision-maker simply WILL NOT approve it on the day of its presentation.

The psychological conundrum equating delay and deliberation with lost money (opportunity) can be a powerful catalyst for some decision-makers.

People tend to support and promote that which they have helped to create and develop.

When developing and communicating the "Estimated Timeline" to the decision-maker—ALWAYS PAD THE NUMBERS!

CHAPTER 12

HOW DIFFICULT WILL IT BE TO IMPLEMENT?

Plan, Communicate, Execute

It was one of the more honest calls I've ever received. So direct and honest, it initially caught me off guard. For 30 years, I'd sold my leadership expertise to business leaders who wanted or needed it. For 30 years, I'd worked to help leaders become more effective and influential. For 30 years, I'd developed theories, systems, and processes; written articles and books; recorded videos; and delivered countless speeches and training sessions on the topic. After 30 years, I thought I'd probably seen and heard it all from a leadership perspective. But I hadn't. As a result of that call, my leadership message became even more focused. The call went something like this:

Me: *"Good morning, Van Hooser Associates."*

Caller: *"Is this Phillip Van Hooser?"*

The voice was male, the tone emphatic.

Me: *"Yes, it is."*

Caller: *"Are you the one who does leadership speeches and training?"*

His no-nonsense directness captured my full attention.

Me: *"Yes, I am."*

Caller: *"You were recommended by someone I trust. I own a business. I've got a bunch of dysfunctional managers and supervisors working for me. They need to be better leaders. Frankly, I need to be a better leader. They need help and so do I."*

My entrepreneurial focus immediately shifted to high alert.

BUSINESS OPPORTUNITY!! BUSINESS OPPORTUNITY!! I thought.

He continued:

Caller: *"But I'm gonna tell you straight up. I'm not hiring you. I don't know what you charge. It doesn't matter. I can't afford it. Now you can hang up on me right now if you want. I'd understand. I'm just calling because my friend encouraged me to do so. He told me you'd shoot straight. He told me you'd help if you could. So there it is. Anything you can do?"*

The caller's point was direct, succinct, and effectively made. It was not the type of business call I usually received. Frankly, I wasn't sure how to respond.

Me: *"Well, I think you've made yourself and your situation clear. Like you, I'm a business owner, and as a business owner, I'm not in the habit of giving my products and services away to everyone who calls. That seems like a good business plan for not being in business very long."*

I forced a chuckle, hoping my feeble attempt at humor would lighten the conversational mood. It didn't.

Caller: *"Yeah, I get it. Sorry to have bothered you."*

Me: *"Wait, wait a minute, don't hang up."*

Caller: *"I'm still here."*

Me: *"In all fairness, you asked me a direct question. A direct question deserves a direct answer. So I'm gonna give you one. But I'm also gonna be straight with you. Don't expect a lot of extra detail. If you want more of what I'm about to give you here, you'll have to pay for it."*

Caller: *"Fair enough. I'm listening."*

With my statement made, I now faced my second problem. I was willing to be direct, but I was totally unsure of what my now-promised "direct answer" should be. I wanted to be of some help. I really did. After all, that's my professional calling—to help leaders lead more effectively.

But how can I do that right now? What do I have to offer in this moment? I wondered.

In the few seconds I had to prepare a response, my mind raced. The task initially seemed impossible. But from somewhere deep in my psyche, summoned, I suppose, by a combination of desperation and determination, a foundational truth bubbled to the surface. Instinctively, I spoke.

Me: *"Over time I've discovered three things great leaders do consistently well. They may seem simple, but they're not. Few leaders practice them, fewer still master them. But those who do end up being the great leaders we long to follow and, hopefully, long to be.*

"First, the most effective leaders plan meticulously. They don't trust their ability to figure things out in the moment. They realize that for important tasks, processes should be planned carefully and intentionally.

"Second, effective leaders purposefully communicate their plans to all who have reason or need to know. They don't assume others have ready access to necessary information or understand it if they do. They provide background information, necessary instruction, and share reasons for their actions.

"Finally, the most effective leaders are determined to fully execute, to follow through on the plans they've made and communicated. When necessary, they adapt and improvise. But effective leaders never abandon the plan just because it's new, difficult, or is taking longer than expected. They finish what they start."

That was it. That's what I shared. I added that I hoped my thoughts had been helpful in some way. He said they had. We exchanged best wishes. Our one and only conversation ended amicably.

Whether the caller was helped that day, I don't know. But I do know—I'd been helped. Our brief, unplanned conversation forced me to synthesize the very essence of what I believed about effective, foundational leadership.

Personal influence as employed by leaders, is rarely, if ever, the by-product of haphazard actions. Influence, trust, respect, and opportunity all result from important tasks carefully planned, clearly communicated, and consistently executed.

The process being explored here is no different. When embarking on *Earning the Right to Be Heard*, the process should be considered one of your most important personal and/or professional leadership undertakings, regardless of the position you occupy. In a very real sense, your future ability to influence others depends in large part on how you lead in and through this process. Utilizing

Influence, trust, respect, and opportunity all result from important tasks carefully planned, clearly communicated, and consistently executed.

this process as designed equips you to plan, communicate, and execute skillfully. Learn and do those three things well and good things can be expected.

The Biggest Challenge Yet

For many new *Earning the Right to Be Heard* practitioners, preparations for responding to the fourth question are often considered to be the toughest yet. This is especially true the first time or two, as individuals begin thinking through and preparing their "Recommended Implementation Plan."

Being unable to foresee or predict the full range of positive opportunities embedded in Question #4, some individuals hesitate, then resist moving forward. Because the process seems tedious, some are tempted to abandon it altogether. If/when they do move ahead, too many skip one or more of the recommended steps. They assume doing so will have little material effect on their ability to respond successfully to the IMPLE-MENTATION question when it comes. But they're wrong—seriously wrong.

With these thoughts in mind, we will consider Question #4 even more deliberately. As is true in many situations in life, successfully overcoming significant hurdles can yield great, often unexpected rewards. For example, preparing a comprehensive "Recommended Implementation Plan" proof, although often challenging, accomplishes two significant steps in our *Earning the Right to Be Heard* process.

First, the "Recommended Implementation Plan" proof provides the most tangible evidence available of one's worthiness to be listened to, valued, and ultimately heard from again and again. The ability and willingness to create a working plan, then communicate that plan skill-fully, is no small accomplishment. It represents tangible evidence of the initiator's skill, preparation, logic, personal drive, and commitment to the initiative.

Second, the "Recommended Implementation Plan" proof may end up serving as the central "working blueprint" supporting the final execution of the initiative if/once approved. A decision-maker's approval and acceptance of the "Recommended Implementation Plan" (with or without additions or omissions) is the most obvious acknowledgment of one's personal elevation in that decision-maker's view regarding trust, respect, and individual influence.

Too Much May Not Be Enough

The importance of Question #4 (IMPLEMENTATION) cannot be overstated. Get this one right and you move to the fifth question and a decision—hopefully, a decision that favors both your primary and secondary objectives. Momentum is building. Unfortunately, I must pause the process momentarily to beg your forgiveness—in advance.

Earlier it was explained that acceptable proofs for the questions under consideration normally require no more than one page of documentation. That's still true. In general, brevity is the most impactful approach. However, to properly answer the IMPLEMENTATION question by including a "Proposed Project Organizational Chart" and a "Project Communication Strategy" (tools introduced in the section to follow), an exception to the "one-page rule" occasionally must be made.

By including this additional (and necessary) information, your implementation proof may expand to a second, possibly even a third page.

That's perfectly okay, as long as these tools contain immediately relevant information. By this point, the decision-maker is actively engaged. They are trusting you to supply complete answers to their questions. Certainly sharing too much information can be a problem, but not sharing enough detail to allow a well-informed decision to be made is a mistake as well.

It's Not My Job

Over the years, the "Recommended Implementation Plan," made up of two parts (the "Proposed Project Organization Chart" and the "Project Communication Strategy"), has been introduced in workshop settings to individuals, groups, and organizations. In such intimate settings, the implementation proof has occasionally been met with resistance. Digging deeper and asking why has revealed a consistent response.

"I had the idea for this initiative. I offered it," says a resistant team member. "I'm even willing to share the idea's credit with my decision-maker and others. But I can't understand why I should I be expected to do all the implementation planning work, too. That's just not my job."

Unfortunately, such a statement is the first step leading down a slippery slope. Although many may not recognize it in the moment, saying/believing, "It's not my job" generally marks the beginning of the imminent failure of that individual's *Earning the Right to Be Heard* quest. Such a mindset not only short-circuits the continuation and growth of an individual's personal influence, but it most likely restricts the person from realizing most objectives they hoped to secure. It's unfortunate. It's also avoidable.

The simple answer to the "How difficult will it be to implement?" question is that it shouldn't be difficult at all. Not difficult, that is, if someone simply commits to planning, communicating, and executing the implementation plan up front. With an effective plan in place, buoyed by unwavering individual commitment, the only thing lacking is decision-maker approval. With approval secured, the initiative can move forward with an exceptionally strong likelihood of long-term success.

But lacking individual commitment—even if/once decision-maker approval has been secured—the initiative is invariably DOA (dead on arrival). Equally lifeless, though not blatantly apparent, is the trust, respect, and influence the decision-maker once had for the person who introduced the initiative. Again, it's unfortunate and avoidable.

Why am I so committed to individual team members stepping up and taking the lead, start to finish, on initiatives for which they have real passion? My commitment is rooted in countless conversations I've had with decision-makers and leaders over the years.

Consider the following exchange as an example. It's a practical representation of dozens of past conversations. The conversation begins with a rather simple question asked of key decision-makers (i.e., presidents, VPs, general managers, right on down to department managers and floor supervisors).

Me: *"Is there at least one project you'd really like to see happen?"*

Decision-Maker: *"Just one? Definitely. In fact, I have many on my wish list."*

Me: *"Would these projects be advantageous to your organization?"*

Decision-Maker: *"Absolutely. Each could provide many benefits."*

Me: *"Are these projects you can afford financially?"*

Decision-Maker: *"Of course. Money is rarely the main obstacle to getting important projects done."*

Me: *"It's not?"*

Decision-Maker: *"Of course not. The biggest problem with getting new projects underway and completed is actually bandwidth. There are always more critical projects to be done than committed people available to oversee them. Single individuals don't possess enough bandwidth individually to start and oversee every new project and still stay on top of everything else that's going on."*

Me: *"So what's the answer?"*

Decision-Maker: *"We need to figure out ways of getting more people to recognize the needs and opportunities that exist. Then those people need to step up and take ownership of those projects. When that happens, things get done and even better things usually follow."*

I've been involved in some version of this conversation literally dozens of times over the years. Unquestionably, these many conversations have shaped my thinking concerning the need to engage more people in more worthwhile projects. The end results are good for the organization and good for those who seize the opportunities. That's why I am such a proponent of *Earning the Right to Be Heard.* The win–win opportunities are virtually limitless.

How Difficult Will It Be to Implement?

A track coach is sure to encourage runners to "run PAST the finish line" in every competitive race. The same concept holds true here. Just as a runner can fall short of the objective by failing to push through to the end, it's equally possible for an individual to come up short in the *Earning the Right to Be Heard* process by slacking off in his or her preparations for Question #4.

With Question #4, our *Earning the Right to Be Heard* race has entered—or is at least approaching—the home stretch. The finish line is in sight, but we're not there yet. We've got to keep pushing. Two important questions remain to be answered.

Mr. Malek's 4th Question:

"Brenda, I appreciate your efforts on this project. What you've done is impressive. The proofs you've prepared have been very helpful. But I must admit, I have a concern. We've got a lot of projects underway, and you've got a lot on your plate. If I approve this initiative, how can I be sure this copier project won't get lost in the shuffle?"

Brenda's Transitional Statement:

"Mr. Malek, there is a lot going on. But this copier project is important for people in the Sales, Marketing, and Service departments who need it now. This 'Recommended Implementation Plan' contains my ideas for how to make this happen with the least amount of confusion."

The "Implementation" Proof

SUNDIAL COPIER RECOMMENDED IMPLEMENTATION PLAN

(Fictional Example)

OVERVIEW/PROJECT RECAP HIGHLIGHTS

"Estimated Cost Analysis" Review (NOTE: Overview from Proof #1)

Direct Costs: $18,562.50
Indirect Costs: $1,562.50
Total Project Cost: $20,125.00

"Estimated Benefits" Review (NOTE: Overview from Proof #2)

Total Benefits Identified (19)
Select Benefits Highlighted Below (11)

Economic Benefits

- Reduced maintenance/repair costs
- Guaranteed 5-year "no question trade-in or buy back" option

Organizational Benefits

- User security authentication (for access to confidential documents)
- Remote access (for employees working remotely or traveling)

Efficiency Benefits

- Significant productivity increases (22 printed pages per minute)
- High-quality custom printing (proposals, annual reports, marketing materials)

Environmental Benefits

- "Energy Savers" technology (environmentally friendly commitment)
- Reduced toner usage (25% reduction expected compared to current usage)

"Estimated Timeline" Review (NOTE: Overview from Proof #3)

Stage 1: Purchase Approval/PO: 4 calendar days
Stage 2: Order, Shipping, Delivery, Setup: 18 calendar days
Stage 3: User Training: 6 calendar days
Stage 4: Copier Available/Full Utilization: 34 total days

OVERVIEW/"RECOMMENDED IMPLEMENTATION PLAN"

"Proposed Project Organization Chart"

Sundial Copier/Project Team:

Project Chair: Brenda
Purchasing Support: Daphne
Human Resources/Training: Tyler
Administrative Support: Melissa

Project Team/General Responsibilities:

Project Manager: Complete project oversight
Purchasing Support: Create/oversee purchasing contract
  Create purchasing order (other documentation)
HR/Training: Secure "user training" training site
  Create/communicate "user training" schedule
Administrative Support: Serve as onsite copier "expert"
  Create copier training metrics (w/ manufacturing rep)

"Proposed Project Communication Strategy"

Phase 1: Project introduction (upon securing project approval)

- Project Manager
  - Within 1 business day of project approval:
    - Contact individual project team members (Purchasing, HR/Training, Administration)
    - Communicate individual project responsibilities
    - Communicate project timelines
- E-mail department managers (Marketing, Sales, and Service)
  - Within 2 business days of project approval:
    - Communicate features of Sundial HVP LaserPro 1957 P-Series copier
    - Announce overall project time schedule
    - Request names of employees to be included in "user training"

Phase 2: Project implementation

- Project Manager
  - Weekly: Update decision-maker as to project's progress
- Purchasing Support
  - Within 3 business days of project approval:
    - Review copier purchase contract
    - Execute official purchase order
  - Weekly:
    - Communicate with copier sales rep to assure expected performance
    - Report progress (or delays) to project manager
- HR/Training
  - Within 7 business days of project approval:
    - Secure "user training" training site
  - Within 10 business days of project approval:
    - Create and communicate "user training" schedule/location
    - Schedule participants for "user training"

- Weekly:
  - Report progress (or delays) to project manager
- Administrative Support
  - Within 10 business days of project approval:
    - Review Sundial HVP LaserPro 1957 P-Series Copier "Operations Manual"
    - Create "user training" metrics, including…
      - Frequently asked questions
      - Shut down and start up basics
      - General "HELP" processes
      - PM (preventative maintenance) schedule
- Weekly:
  - Report progress (or delays) to project manager

Phase 3: Project debriefing

- Within 3 business days of project completion:
  - Project manager to conduct final "review meeting" with Mr. Malek
  - Discuss final project costs
  - Discuss "user training" review
    - General review:
      - What went well?
      - What went poorly?
      - Who needs commendation for project performance?
      - What should be done differently in the future?

Overview/Project Highlights

The first section of the "Recommended Implementation Plan" should look familiar. It contains an abbreviated review of information contained in the cost, benefit, and time proofs. These informative snapshots are presented in an intentionally scaled-down format designed to provide decision-makers a quick "side-by-side" review of information already discussed. The information to be highlighted (i.e., total cost, premier benefits, overall timelines) is completely determined by the originator of the initiative.

Overview/Recommended Implementation Plan

The "Recommended Implementation Plan" melds cost, benefit, and time highlights with two additional comprehensive sections: "Project Organization Chart" and "Project Communication Strategy."

Project Organization Chart

Decision-makers en masse agree that a continuing need exists to have team members at all levels become more engaged in project/initiative identification, development, and execution. Such agreement encourages individual team members to offer personal suggestions—including the creation, formation, and organization of ad hoc project teams. Of course, decision-makers and key personnel always retain final decision-making authority regarding any matter involving team members. However, the

"Project Organization Chart" provides an opportunity to make and defend suggestions for the involvement and engagement of fellow team members in ways that may not have been considered previously.

When considering how a project might be organized, there are a few basic questions that can help point the way. Such questions might include:

- Who would be best suited to lead the implementation of this project?

- Who is well-informed concerning the details of this initiative?

- Who has skill sets that might align nicely with the needs of this initiative?

- Who should get involved so that leaders can gauge their future performance capabilities?

Projects generally run more smoothly when team members are asked to do what they are already skilled at doing. Your ability to effectively identify, enlist, and assign team members to specific tasks in the project will not go unnoticed by key decision-makers.

One other point regarding organizational decisions. As you consider specific positional assignments (when appropriate), be sure that suggestions for placements are carefully explained to decision-makers and are NEVER based on ego—yours or others. There may be occasions when your proposed organization chart (one you have developed) positions you as "chair" or in the lead position. On another occasion your organization chart (again, one you have developed) might recommend that someone else take the lead and you function in a lesser position. The priority assignments should always go to those individuals most capable of performing them most effectively.

Project Communication Strategy

When looking to identify one professional habit to develop that is guaranteed to pay dividends throughout your career, look no further than personal communication skill enhancement. The ability to effectively communicate different messages, to different individuals (or audiences), utilizing different communication media is a skill that never goes out of style or loses favor. As you consciously and strategically heighten your communication skill levels, continuously look to apply those expanding skills by creating new, proactive communication strategies. Commit to creating a strategic communication approach, then use it habitually.

Over the years I've been amazed at how many key leaders and decision-makers complain both publicly and privately regarding how little they know about what's going on in their organizations. It's not that they don't want to know. They do. It's that others, those people "in the know" (often on the front lines), make little to no effort to share timely updates and ongoing developments.

Consider this representative statement. I've heard it time and again, in one iteration or another, from even top decision-makers.

"When asked specific questions about activities happening under my watch, one of two things often happens: I either have to pretend I know more than I do, or I have to start calling people to find out what's really going on. Neither situation is a comfortable one. It's frustrating. I wish people understood how helpful and appreciated regular updates would be."

The ability to effectively communicate different messages, to different individuals (or audiences), utilizing different communication media is a skill that never goes out of style or loses favor.

This is what's known as a "correctable error." No one is suggesting information is intentionally being withheld from the decision-maker. Certainly not me. People get busy, priorities get scrambled, attention gets drawn elsewhere, and the unintentional by-product of it all is that communication suffers. But this problem can be corrected.

When that decision-maker clearly states what their frustrations are, as well as what would eliminate those frustrations, an opportunity has presented itself. The person who proactively steps up to make those frustrations go away is going to be noticed. Contrary to what others may think or say, this is NOT about "sucking up." It's about being a professional, a team player, and a problem solver. Prove yourself to be all three to decision-makers and the chances of you selling your ideas, building your influence, and growing your opportunities increase accordingly.

To be more proactive in your *Earning the Right to Be Heard* communications, here are two simple suggestions.

One, on a regular basis (weekly, biweekly, or at the very least monthly) casually make a point of telling your key decision-maker what you've been up to. Tell them what you're working on, how it's going, and what stage of the process (development or completion) you are currently in—all before they are forced to ask.

Two, better still, let them know you are planning to institute a slightly more formal "activity report" in which you will be communicating issues of interest to them and others. Ask the decision-maker if there is anything in particular they would like you to include and what format is preferable for sharing the updates. Then follow through.

Remember, it's hard to communicate too much—but incredibly easy to communicate too little.

Hypersensitivity Is Nonsense

There is one final point to be made regarding the creation and ownership of these suggested individualized implementation plans. It's an important one.

Let's assume you do everything right. You spend the appropriate time up front creating a solid "Recommended Implementation Plan," including a carefully thought-out "Project Organization Chart" and a well-defined "Project Communication Strategy." Once the decision-maker asks you the IMPLEMENTATION question, you're ready. You present these comprehensive implementation plans and proof for their consideration.

Upon careful review, the plans are met with great enthusiasm. The decision-maker is especially excited to finally discover an individual who "gets it." You've made great, bold strides in their eyes. The decision-maker's genuine enthusiasm gives way to professional support. Almost immediately, they become both an advocate and an ally. They encourage the forward movement of the project.

As the project moves forward, good things begin to happen. Others in the organization begin to notice and comment on the many benefits being realized. The initiative currently underway is shaping up to be an unqualified success.

Then one day in a heavily populated meeting, a specific question is asked by one attendee regarding the initiative. The decision-maker voluntarily fields the question and responds:

"I appreciate your question. A number of you have commented recently on the initiative currently underway. I want to say publicly how much I appreciate the work of the implementation team to make this initiative a reality. When I first sat down and began to consider all the positive benefits

associated with this project, envisioning the implementation plan necessary to make it all work..."

Suddenly, you feel your face flush and your pulse quicken. As the decision-maker continues with their comments, you begin to shift uncomfortably in your seat. While looking down at the table in front of you, you feel your blood pressure rising.

How dare they! you rage internally. *That implementation plan was 100 percent my idea! Now here they are trying to take credit for MY idea—and they're doing it with me sitting RIGHT HERE! If I don't do something, they'll take all the credit. Well, I'm not gonna let them get away with it.*

Stop right there before you do or say something you're sure to regret. Please just think through this with me. At this moment, while you're still in a positive, receptive frame of mind, let me remind you of a few very important facts.

First, the project you initiated is underway. The implementation plan is working as intended. Don't forget that. And don't forget that you couldn't have done that alone. Be happy that your plan met with such enthusiastic approval from the decision-maker in the first place. That doesn't always happen. Without the decision-maker's initial enthusiasm and support, your project most likely would've never gotten off the ground. Let your decision-maker celebrate the project's success, whether publicly or privately, as they choose. It's a good thing for both of you.

Second, in the midst of your initial frustration, you may be tempted to "set the record straight." Please resist that terrible temptation. There is NOTHING—repeat NOTHING—good that can come from you "calling out" your decision-maker publicly. No one needs to know that you resent them taking credit for your work. It's a really dangerous—and foolish—thing to do. Don't lean over and whisper privately to the person sitting next to you in the meeting. Don't go out and complain publicly to a group gathered in the break room later. For heaven's sake, don't share your aggravation via social media—even if the names are changed or omitted entirely. Just don't do it.

But why not? What the decision-maker is doing is not right, you may be thinking. *They shouldn't be able to get away with it.*

If you will, try to think of this situation from a slightly different angle. If the decision-maker is actually taking credit for your work, then you can be sure of one thing: they like your work. They certainly wouldn't take credit for flawed work, would they? Instead, they'd be looking for someone to blame, which they're certainly not doing.

In fact, they're probably no longer thinking of it as exclusively *your* work or even *their* work. By this point in the project, in their mind it's become a team effort. It's no longer *yours* or *theirs*; it's become *our* project, *our* work.

That line of thinking makes perfect sense if you think about it. You presented the idea to the decision-maker initially. They listened and carefully evaluated the pros and cons of your presentation. Eventually, they came around to your way of thinking, and as you wished, they approved your request. That process has worked well for both of you!

With their approval secured, you set about putting the implementation plan to work—and now it's working. On a foundational level, the decision-maker is justified in thinking of this overall project from a joint ownership perspective. They are in it right up to their ears with you. Be happy you've got a supportive partner. Don't let your ego cause you to ruin a good thing.

Think of it this way: if your decision-maker chooses to co-opt your idea(s) as their own, that person has invested in you, and in their eyes, your "personal stock" is "up and rising." When you do something so well that someone else—especially a decision-maker—wishes to be a part of it, then your personal influence is clearly at work.

If, on the other hand, you choose to embarrass that decision-maker publicly by "calling them out" or undercutting their efforts in front of others, you can fully expect your "personal stock" to drop like a rock. Regardless of the success of the one project currently underway, you are no longer likely to get what you want in the future. Worse still, the process of *Earning the Right to Be Heard* for you going forward will quickly come to a grinding halt.

If/when someone, especially a decision-maker, takes more credit than you think is deserved for work you've done, take a deep breath, smile, raise your head, then take it all in stride and keep on doing good work. Others are watching. Others are more aware than you might think. Others will soon take note without you ever having to tell them (or anyone) anything. Your attitude, your efforts, and, most importantly, your results will do all the talking necessary.

A Concise Review

Personal influence is rarely, if ever, the by-product of haphazard actions. Influence, trust, respect, and opportunity all result from important tasks carefully planned, clearly communicated, and confidently executed.

The ability and willingness to create a working implementation plan, then communicate that plan, represents tangible evidence of the author's intelligence, skill, preparation, logic, rationale, and personal commitment to the initiative.

Commit to creating a proactive communication strategic approach, then use it habitually.

When you do something so well that someone else—especially a decision-maker—wishes to be a part of it, then your personal influence is clearly at work.

CHAPTER 13

WHAT ARE THE POSSIBLE CONSEQUENCES?

Expect the Unexpected

Chapter by chapter, section by section, the purpose of this book has remained consistent: to offer a practical, step-by-step process by which individuals can effectively prepare and present ideas and initiatives to decision-makers for consideration and action. In accomplishing this purpose, individuals can expect personal influence and new opportunities to build and grow.

Simple concept. Streamlined process. Assured outcome? Not so fast.

The concept *is* simple, and the process *is* streamlined. But even simple, streamlined processes encounter resistance from time to time. Unexpected, unplanned resistance often results in a slowing of the process, frustrating detours, and unanticipated pressures. Each requires due attention and appropriate action. But while in the midst of frustrating occurrences, the desired outcome may become blurred and not so assured after all.

As a young HR supervisor, I was responsible for facilitating monthly "Employee Roundtable Discussions" for my company. Each session involved six employees, the operation's manager, and me. Face time with the operation's manager was a big deal. These sessions allowed employees to ask questions, voice concerns, and share ideas openly and directly with *the* key decision-maker. My role was simply to arrange the meetings, serve as the scribe, and attend to other duties as directed.

My primary "as directed" duty was to make available a post-meeting synopsis of topics/responses discussed for general employee review. Topics needing more in-depth attention and explanation than could be provided in the meeting were forwarded to the appropriate department head (finance, purchasing, operations, etc.) for his/her written response. With all responses in hand, I would distribute the compiled information, always inside a promised ten-day window post-meeting. The operation's manager referred to it as our "ten-day commitment."

As designed, the process worked well. Until it didn't. After months of faultless execution, we experienced our first fail on our "ten-day commitment." The engineering manager had failed to return his written responses in time. Not my problem.

Nevertheless, on that critical eleventh day, while standing outside my office, I saw the operation's manager approaching. I greeted him. He skipped the pleasantries and demanded to know why the responses hadn't been distributed. My explanation, including pointing fingers, did no good. My responsibility was explained to me again in no uncertain terms. The ten-day promise was mine to keep.

Naturally, I was upset. At first, I was embarrassed. But my embarrassment quickly turned to frustration, then to straight-up anger. The engineering manager was to blame, not me. So, once free from the operation's manager's wrath, I decided to tell him so. I headed directly to the true culprit's office, never pausing to think, seeking to understand, or preparing to respond. I just reacted. Emotionally.

Not so surprisingly, before I could get back to my office following this "encounter" with the engineering manager, my manager intercepted me. Bad news traveled quickly in our office. I then received my second stern "talking-to" in less than ten minutes' time. A record, even for me.

Calmly but directly, my boss explained that all decision-makers deserved respect and professional consideration for the difficult jobs they do—even engineering managers. He pointed out that I had never paused to consider his point of view, I had never offered my help, and I had done nothing to anticipate or prepare for the possibility of a missed deadline. He assured me that such events would happen again. Unfortunate outcomes will always be with us. He wondered out loud what my next response might be. He hoped it would be more proactive and positive than my prior move. He concluded by reminding me that building influence was hard; rebuilding, harder still.

Unintended Consequences

Yes, unforeseen occurrences will happen—regularly—even daily. But as has been said by many before me, it's not what happens to you that matters most; it's what you do with and about what happens to you. If unforeseen occurrences are handled poorly or haphazardly, unintended consequences (usually negative) can be the unfortunate result.

Unintended consequences are real and common. As such, they should be anticipated and planned for intentionally. But know this: your personal fear of unintended, unforeseen consequences should NEVER be allowed to restrict your forward progress. You cannot afford to surrender both your influence and future potential to two overrated fears: the fear of the unknown and the fear of failure.

When presented with a new concept or opportunity, even one as promising and proven as *Earning the Right to Be Heard*, it's not unusual for idea sellers to be tempted to pause. "New" anything can elicit an inclination toward extreme caution, including downright reluctance to proceed, in some. Though these actions/reactions may provide the appearance of safety and security in the moment, forward progress has been impeded. In order to advance in the *Earning the Right to Be Heard* process, the true danger of unintended consequences needs to be acknowledged and overcome.

Opportunities, Complacency, Execution

As you anticipate being asked Question #5, you may begin to consider its relative magnitude. It may seem as if the outcome of this entire process balances precariously on your answer to this one, final question. That's not completely true. Had you not anticipated, prepared, and responded well to the first four questions, you would never have made it to Question #5.

But it's not completely untrue either. Question #5 is important. The outcome of the process is still in question. Therefore, your response to

Question #5 bears great weight—great enough that it must not be taken for granted.

In this final homestretch of the process, you are encouraged to keep three important points in mind: 1) always look for opportunities, 2) avoid complacency, and 3) execute the process completely.

Look for opportunities. The entire *Earning the Right to Be Heard* process has been carefully developed and documented for your benefit. Predictable questions have been named, correct answers have been identified, appropriate attitudes have been specified. Every attempt has been made to highlight every available opportunity necessary for accomplishing your objectives. Guess what? We missed some.

Real-time process interactions are similar to people—every one unique. You're sure to encounter unique situations, unique circumstances, unique timing, unique personalities, unique requests, and so forth. Don't be surprised or dismayed when something different—unique—happens. Those are opportunities. Be quick to identify unique opportunities, each readymade for you to showcase your imagination, creativity, ingenuity, and desire to make important things happen.

For example, don't forgo the opportunity to ask decision-makers questions, such as: *Do you mind sharing your greatest concern? What would keep you from acting on this request? How might I have better presented this initiative for your consideration?* In other words, never stop looking for and pursuing the opportunities available to accomplish your objectives.

Avoid complacency. Countless speakers, writers, educators, and philosophers throughout history have shared deep, probing thoughts and concerns regarding the topic of human complacency and the real dangers of succumbing to its temptations. Complacency kills imagination, creativity, ingenuity, desire—the actual opportunities mentioned previously that influence-seekers embrace and pursue.

Be forewarned: a complacent mindset will pose questions such as these: *How can I be sure this process will work? Shouldn't I wait until I know it works for someone else before trying it? What will it hurt to wait another week? Month? Year?*

Insidious self-talk and self-questioning, if allowed to continue, can lead to duplicitous tricks being played on one's own mind. Recognize complacency and the negative-leaning mindsets for what they are—dangerous. Consciously resist both. Fight your way through them. Otherwise, the ravages of a complacent attitude—smugness, self-satisfaction, mediocrity—may be visited upon you, none of which serve to advance your objective of *Earning the Right to Be Heard.*

Execute the process effectively. Earlier in this book, a story was shared about an individual seeking leadership advice and help. The help offered was a threefold recommendation: plan, communicate, and execute. That advice still holds. To realize the full benefit of this process, one must do all three. None of these steps in isolation will singularly enable you to be heard or to accomplish your objectives. Each must be embraced and employed in combination with equal commitment and enthusiasm to realize the benefits of the process. Unfortunately, one of these three attributes too often gets short shrift: execution.

Many people plan (formally and/or informally) and communicate (talk about their plans). However, too many of them fail to embrace the execution part. They falter when it comes time to put their words and plans into action. Conversely, the most successful people I know, in every imaginable field or enterprise, are those who consciously double down on attitude, technique, and execution in all that they do.

WHAT ARE THE POSSIBLE CONSEQUENCES?

The Parable of the Talents

For thousands of years, parables have been used to communicate abiding, universal truths. Parables are effective learning tools that employ a short story to illustrate an important lesson or principle. Parables follow a familiar structure. A dilemma of some sort is highlighted, resulting in a decision (good and/or bad), which yields some unintended consequence. Within that parable resides underlying lessons regarding how people should ultimately act, think, or behave.

The "Parable of the Talents" can be found in the biblical book of Matthew (chapter 25, verses 14–30). This parable is a good representation of, among other things, the benefits afforded those who actively look for opportunities, avoid complacency, and execute effectively.

This parable begins by detailing a certain man's preparations before embarking on an extended journey. He arranges to have his valuables (talents) looked after during his upcoming absence by three trusted servants. To each servant he assigns an individual task. To the first servant he entrusts the care of five talents; to a second servant, two talents; and to a third servant, only one talent.

The story continues. Once the man had departed on his journey, the first two servants took what had been entrusted to their care (five and two talents, respectively) and began wise business dealings. The story tells us their "trades" resulted in both servants doubling what they began with. Five talents became ten, and two talents became four. But the third servant responded very differently. The third servant took his one talent and buried it in the ground and left it there for presumed safekeeping.

Eventually, the rightful owner returned to collect his talents. Upon discovering that the first two servants had doubled what he had previously entrusted to them, he was overjoyed. He heaped lavish praise on them, before elevating their status (their influence), putting them both "in charge of many things" (opportunities).

But the third servant experienced a different outcome. He returned his one talent to the man, admitting that he had been afraid of the man's response had he lost the one talent. He had taken what appeared to be the safest possible action to protect it from possible loss: he had buried the talent. In doing nothing productive with it, he squandered both the time and talent available to him. Having done nothing, he could not gain anything.

The parable concludes by stating the owner of the talent was displeased with the actions of the third servant and therefore took the third servant's talent and gave it to the first servant.

In a contemporary manner, this parable has tentacles that extend beyond the centuries and into organizations today. Organizations entrust employees with the care and safekeeping of valuable organizational resources (i.e., material resources, financial resources, customer resources, etc.). These employees enjoy equal opportunity to utilize and employ available resources for the continuing good of the organization. In the end, some take advantage of the available opportunities, and some don't. Those who do generally reap increased influence and enlarged opportunities, while those who could have, but didn't, don't. While the latter group often laments their circumstances, just as often they disregard the fact that their situation is of their own making.

Proof Free

Before I go further, here's a bit of good news: there are no more proofs to be developed. YAY! Right?

Unlike Questions #1 through #4, Question #5 does not require an independent proof to serve as a document of support. Previously developed proofs ("Estimated Cost Analysis," "Estimated Benefits," "Estimated Timeline," and "Recommended Implementation Plan") are still important. They will continue to play a prominent role as this process approaches its logical climax.

For example, don't be surprised if, during closing discussions, a decision-maker references one or more previous proof(s). He/she may have lingering questions that a former proof might answer. In that situation, a quick review of the previous proofs might be in order. Just know that the proofs already completed and introduced will continue to provide ready support whenever documentation is appropriate. But again, no new proof for Question #5 is necessary.

What Are the Consequences of Not Taking Action?

Mr. Malek's 5th Question:

"Brenda, the way you've introduced this initiative has been impressive. Your preparation, the efficient use of our time, the introduction of the proofs—it's all been well done.

"I admit, a new copier is a worthy request. But there are other worthy requests to be considered. I must ask: What are the consequences of not taking action?"

The Three Don'ts

The statement above is just about the LAST thing an idea seller wants to hear from a decision-maker at this stage. This is especially true considering the significant time and energy already invested in researching, preparing, and presenting the initiative. The proposed idea is worthy. You know that. The benefits of the initiative have been defended and legitimized.

But before sharing what *should be done* in response to Question #5, there are three definite things that *should not be done.* They are simply 1) don't overreact, 2) don't fear rejection, and 3) don't shrink from the challenge.

Don't overreact. That moment in which a decision-maker gives even the slightest indication that he/she might be considering doing nothing in response to your requested initiative is a critical one. How you respond may prove to be that "make-or-break" moment for the entire interaction.

If you overreact verbally (*"You can't be serious!"*) or nonverbally (*drawing a ragged sigh, rolling your eyes, slumping noticeably in your chair*), you can rightly expect some related emotional reaction or response from the decision-maker, as well. Therefore, at this stage of the process, you simply can't afford to overreact.

Don't fear rejection. Any indication that a decision-maker might not decide in your favor or that he/she might choose to take no action at all must not be interpreted as a personal rejection of you or your efforts. Remember, decision-makers are constantly striving to make decisions on the basis of logic.

By now you've presented plenty of good information worthy of careful consideration. This decision is shaping up to be a weighty one—possibly

WHAT ARE THE POSSIBLE CONSEQUENCES?

more so than was initially expected by the decision-maker. There's a lot riding on it. Both you and the decision-maker understand that. Just keep in mind, whatever the decision-maker's ultimate decision, the primary objective remains the same—*Earning the Right to Be Heard.*

Don't shrink from the challenge. As has been said many times throughout the preceding pages, you must trust the process! You've made it all the way to Question #5. Therefore, you've done a lot of things right. But you're not finished. Not yet. The biggest challenge looms before you.

There is only one recommended way to respond to Question #5. It involves a concluding statement consisting of two parts. Both parts of this concluding statement must be delivered with intention, sincerity, and confidence.

It may not be the easiest thing you've ever done, but doing it is necessary. This is no time to shrink from the challenge. This is the homestretch. You're so close. Keep your eye on the prize.

A Firm Commitment

Mr. Malek's 5th Question:

"... a new copier is a worthy request. But there are other worthy requests to be considered. I must ask: What are the consequences of not taking action?"

Brenda fully expected Question #5 to be asked, so it did not catch her off guard or upset her. In anticipation of Question #5, Brenda had her two-part concluding statement at the ready.

This two-part statement is designed to be offered sequentially—"Concluding Statement/Part 1" followed after a very brief pause by "Concluding Statement/Part 2." Of its two parts, "Concluding Statement/Part 2" is designed to deliver the greatest impact. However, "Concluding Statement/Part 1" should never be overlooked or taken for granted. As with previous action steps in the *Earning the Right to Be Heard* process, each step has a defined purpose and cannot be omitted.

Brenda's Concluding Statement/Part 1:

"Mr. Malek, I appreciate the difficult decision you must make. I've done everything I could to give you the best information to make the best decision possible.

"Of course, I know there's a chance you might not approve or support this initiative. If that's your decision, I'll be disappointed. But I'm a team player. Whatever your decision, I will continue to support the objectives of the organization."

(Intentional pause)

You must recognize the one predictable concern that weighs heavily on every decision-maker. It involves how an idea initiator might respond to the rejection of his/her idea. If the decision-maker ends up denying the request, what then? What will be the effect on the working relationship with the idea initiator AFTER the decision? Better? Worse? The same?

You can bet decision-makers will be wondering. Will the decision be accepted as intended—as nothing more than a business decision? Or will the team member choose to interpret the rejection as a personal affront? Is a rift between the team member and the decision-maker possible or probable? Will the team member deal with the disappointment privately or share his/her frustrations publicly? Could rejection of this request create a period of demotivation, disgruntlement, even withdrawal and/or aggression?

No decision-maker wants to have to deal with the negative baggage that can accompany hurt feelings. Decision-makers wish to make the best, most informed decision possible for all involved, all the while maintaining the collegiality of the team. They are committed to doing what's right for the organization they represent. Nevertheless, they must be keenly aware of how their decision might be received by the team or individual team member. This is especially true if their decision is expected to be unpopular.

That's why Brenda's "Concluding Statement/Part 1"—a prepared, measured, unemotional response—is so important. It preemptively addresses the decision-maker's unspoken concerns head on. It reassures the decision-maker of continued support and commitment before any final decision is made and communicated.

Brenda's Concluding Statement/Part 1:

> "I appreciate the difficult decision you must make."

Unsolicited, public acknowledgment that you're not just thinking about yourself and what you want is sure to be well received. Sincerely acknowledging the decision-maker for the difficulty of their role in rendering a decision will also be appreciated.

Brenda's Concluding Statement/Part 1:

> "I know there's a chance you might not approve or support this initiative. If that's your decision, I'll be disappointed."

Pretending not to be disappointed is unwise. Claiming not to care whether you get what you want or not is both disingenuous and counterproductive. It sends one of two messages, neither of which is consistent with our stated objectives: either the initiative wasn't as important to you as you indicated previously (therefore, your previous efforts can be viewed as an attempt at manipulation) or you're just flat-out lying about how you're feeling (lying is always wrong). Again, neither of these positions can be viewed as positive if your primary objective is to be heard and to build influence.

The fact is, if rejected, you will be disappointed. Say so. But make sure to say so in a professional manner. Remember, strong working relationships are always anchored in mutual trust and respect.

Brenda's Concluding Statement/Part 1:

> "I'm a team player. Whatever your decision, I will continue to support the objectives of the organization."

Yes, of course you'll be disappointed if you don't get what you want. But you have no intention of sulking, pouting, or quitting. By your words, you acknowledge and accept your dual roles as both a professional and a team player. Your direct comment to that effect, as long as it's honest and sincere, is sure to be received favorably.

Remember, maintaining a harmonious working environment is a central goal of every serious decision-maker. Decision-makers want team players on their team. It's that simple. So, reassure them. Tell them you are a team player. Don't make them wonder. Assure them that you can be counted on—no matter what. They need to hear you say it. They want to hear you say it. They'll be glad to hear you say it.

Benefits, Benefits, Benefits

With "Concluding Statement/Part 1" now delivered, Brenda finds herself in the single most critical moment of the entire *Earning the Right to Be Heard* process. The fifth question has been asked by Mr. Malek and is now half answered by Brenda.

Mr. Malek, having wondered aloud what harm might be done if no particular action is taken on the initiative, is carefully processing and evaluating Brenda's response. He's currently unaware that he's heard only "part 1" of her "concluding statement." Nevertheless, Brenda's brief statement is sure to reassure Mr. Malek of her unmistakable desire to see the initiative approved and enacted. But the statement also serves to reassure Mr. Malek of Brenda's continued commitment to the organization and the team regardless of the final decision.

Then comes "part 2" of Brenda's "concluding statement." Mr. Malek could not have reasonably expected more to come. Therefore, part 2 needs to be intentionally brief and to the point for it to be impactful. It needs to be prepared and delivered with confidence, purpose, poise, and resolve. Here's how that's done.

Brenda's Concluding Statement/Part 2:

"Whatever your decision, I will continue to support the objectives of the organization. However, if you choose not to approve this proposal, please remember the project benefits that will not be realized as a result of your decision today."

The statement is intended to create the following image in the decision-maker's mind:

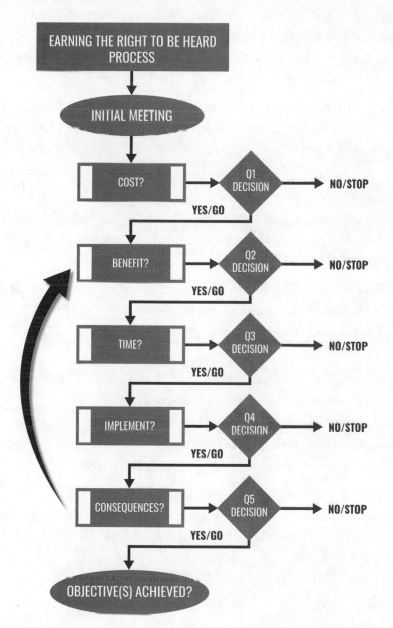

As promised, Brenda's concluding comment is simple, direct, and unwavering. It is not tinged with any sort of inappropriate emotion or a tone that could be interpreted as being aggressive, confrontational, or mean-spirited. Brenda understands what she's saying. Just as importantly, she understands how it should be said and the gravity of the moment. In total, she realizes the importance of getting it all just right.

With her concluding statement, Brenda directs Mr. Malek's attention once more to the benefits listed previously in the Question #2 proof ("Estimated Benefits"), as well as those benefits highlighted in the "Recommended Implementation Plan/Estimated Benefits Review."

Finally, Brenda does the very thing that is so difficult for most of us. Once her carefully prepared response has been skillfully delivered, she shuts up. She intentionally lets her words hang there. She doesn't try to prop them up with more words.

There's really nothing more to be said. Brenda has honestly, directly, and unflinchingly answered every question asked of her. She has provided appropriate commentary when needed. Her presentation is now over with this final comment.

Of course, if Mr. Malek chooses to ask more questions, Brenda will certainly respond to them. But both Brenda and Mr. Malek now realize this process has reached its logical conclusion. The only remaining issue of consequence is the actual decision itself. But of course, the person controlling that step is the decision-maker alone.

As for Brenda, she's concluded her undertaking. She's executed the process from start to finish. She knows she's done what she could do, and regardless of the decision-maker's verdict on her initiative, she can be pleased with her diligent, polished efforts.

A Concise Review

Unintended, unforeseen consequences are real and fairly common. They should be anticipated and planned for as intentionally as possible.

One predictable concern that can be expected to weigh heavily on any decision-maker involves how the idea's initiator might respond to the rejection of his/her idea, which is why it's important to assure the decision-maker of your continued support and commitment to the organization, regardless of his/her verdict.

Pretending not to be disappointed if you don't get what you want is both disingenuous and counterproductive to the future development of a trusting relationship.

The recommended concluding statement is "If you choose not to approve this proposal, please remember the project benefits that will not be realized as a result of your decision today."

SECTION 4:

REALIZING THE PAYOFF

CHAPTER 14

WHAT NOW, WHAT NEXT?

Cliff Hangers or Happy Endings?

Do you prefer cliff hangers or stories with happy endings? Depending on your preference, you may or may not be pleased with how the last chapter ended. Was it too abrupt for your liking? Maybe you haven't yet decided whether Mr. Malek is a good guy or a bad guy. Will that be determined only by whether or not Brenda's request is granted?

As for Brenda, do you think she was too assertive in her closing statement? Or should she have fought harder, defending her initiative even more vigorously?

As for the fate of the proposal, if approved, might Brenda become overconfident, even cocky? If rejected, might she grow detached and indifferent?

Or maybe you're just wondering, *What now and what next?*

The *now* is that we've entered this book's fourth and final section: "Realizing the Payoff." The title indicates *some* payoff is to be expected. But will it be the *expected* payoff?

The intention here is not to overdramatize this process. On the other hand, it's foolish to expect the process to be completely devoid of drama. Let's face facts. As long as the final decision hangs in the balance, there will be a measure of drama. Drama naturally exists where uncertainty resides.

One remaining unknown is how Mr. Malek will respond to Brenda's concluding comment. Her comment clearly placed the burden of responsibility directly in Mr. Malek's lap. As Brenda indicated, his decision will determine whether the initiative's benefits will be realized or forfeited. Undoubtedly, it was a bold step. But did her final remarks improve the chances of getting the copier project approved? And regardless of whether they did or did not yield Brenda the answer she wanted, was the process and her role in it—from start to finish—beneficial in highlighting her and her ideas going forward?

Honestly, we just don't know. Every situation can be expected to be different based on many variables. Without knowing all the context, it's simply unfair to say whether the proposal will ultimately be approved or not.

The *Earning the Right to Be Heard* process is not intended to be a panacea—a one-size-fits-all solution for every difficulty. Each initiative envisioned is unique and should be approached that way. However, although the initiatives may be different, the process remains consistent: do your research; schedule a meeting with the decision-maker; engage your audience with a succinct proposal; build out the rationale for the initiative by answering five key questions, supported by four proof documents; and transfer the responsibility for realizing the initiative's benefits to the decision-maker.

It will always be human nature to "want what you want" from the process, but remember—the short-term "yes" or "no" from the decision-maker is only your secondary objective. Your primary objective is gaining influence and earning future opportunities. For this reason, more important than the immediate result of the process is how you respond *after* the decision-maker communicates his/her decision.

If/when the final decision comes down in your favor, certainly you need to always be gracious and appreciative. NEVER boast about or flaunt your victory as if it were yours alone. Brenda shouldn't brag that she "got our department this copier." To do so could easily create distance, even friction, between her and her colleagues. Unintentionally, she might soon find herself alone on a social island of her own making, segregated from her colleagues due to her attitude.

Even more damaging would be for Brenda to be less than appreciative of Mr. Malek and his role in this process. Truly, without him, a decision-maker willing to listen and take action, the copier wouldn't have been possible. Recognize that. Acknowledge that. There's no need to gush annoyingly about Mr. Malek and his role. But it is appropriate to share with colleagues how Mr. Malek's role made it possible "for all of us" to realize the benefits of the copier. Mr. Malek will appreciate the public acknowledgment (we all would), but more importantly your attitude and actions will continue to support the influence you've earned and Mr. Malek's desire to hear from you again.

But what if the decision is not what you were hoping for? What you choose to do next is even more critical. Remember, deep down all effective decision-makers worry about scenarios in which they must say "no" and what emotional response such a decision might unleash. It's every bit as important to remain logical and rational *after* learning your proposal has been rejected (for whatever reason) than when you were first developing and presenting it. Here are three foundational recommendations on how to do just that.

Be appreciative. Regardless of the outcome and whether you believe the right decision was made or not, be appreciative of the opportunity you had to present your case. Unfortunately, many professionals who desire to make a difference with their thoughts and ideas are never granted an audience with a decision-maker. Their pitch is not welcomed. Admittedly, the *Earning the Right to Be Heard* process offers clear instruction on *how* to request such a meeting professionally. But it's always the decision-maker's call as to whether he/she will participate. If you were fortunate enough to present your idea to the decision-maker, be sure that he/she knows you appreciated the opportunity and haven't taken it for granted.

Request a debriefing. Immediately after a decision has been made, there is a wonderful opportunity to learn even more about how a decision-maker thinks. In this context, a debriefing is a meeting that enables you to retrace your steps in the *Earning the Right to the Be Heard* process and solicit feedback from the decision-maker on how he/she received each element of the program. A debriefing can be requested after any significant decision (positive or negative), but such a meeting tends to be more helpful once you've learned that you won't be getting what you had advocated for. The decision-maker is sure to be impressed that you haven't "given up" and that you are already making an effort to be better prepared the next time.

Here are four appropriate questions to ask during a post-decision debriefing:

1. What did I do well?

2. What could I have done better?

3. What extenuating circumstances affected your decision that I could/should have recognized and controlled?

4. What extenuating circumstances affected your decision that I would have had no control over?

As you did at the beginning of the *Earning the Right to Be Heard* process, you should request a formal meeting time to discuss these questions with the decision-maker. But unlike the first time, fully disclose what you wish to discuss up front: "Now that the decision has been made, I'd like to ask you a few questions in order to learn and grow from this experience."

Seek future direction. Soon after learning of the decision not to support your proposal is an appropriate time for the seller of the idea to seek out actual "next steps." You've now learned you won't be getting what you wanted. Therefore, ask a decision-maker candidly if your idea is completely dead, without hope of resuscitation.

This is an important question. If no possible hope exists for your idea in the future, you should know and accept that. Such knowledge will save you time and aggravation.

But don't expect the decision-maker to offer that insight freely. It's not that he/she is trying to mislead you. Instead, he/she likely doesn't want to add an additional layer of disappointment to your current defeat. But if you ask directly, he/she will be compelled to tell you the truth.

If, in the process, the decision-maker tells you that the idea has some merit but not in its current form, then you can decide your future course of action: to try again or not. But you'll do so with a clearer understanding of what the future holds.

This Is the Beginning

Earning the Right to Be Heard should never be thought of as a "one-and-done" process. This method has a defined starting point but rarely an ending point. It begins with a project or initiative of your own choosing, but regardless of its outcome, the effects of the process won't end there.

Your demonstrated ability to direct and apply the *Earning the Right to Be Heard* process will affect the way decision-makers view you. Once decision-makers recognize your capacity for understanding and applying rational problem-solving techniques to real-world organizational challenges, expect things to be forever changed. But beware: that change can be for better or worse.

If executed properly, the process is bound to provide additional opportunities for your voice, opinion, and influence to be heard and experienced—again and again. In the grand scheme of things, the outcome of this individual initiative matters little. Why? Because it is simply the starting point from which the future will be built—the future of your influence and opportunities.

If executed improperly, you shouldn't expect the process to end there, either. Unfortunately, demonstrating an inability or stubborn unwillingness to grasp and apply a process decision-makers clearly prefer can conversely result in your voice, opinion, and influence being muted indefinitely.

Decision-makers have long memories, strong opinions, and significant influence. They invariably want to know and be aligned with individuals who "get it." Individuals who can clearly define a problem, frame a solution for that problem, then present that solution in a professional, unemotional manner are certain to get additional opportunities to do so.

"Bearing" the Burden

Remember, this *Earning the Right to Be Heard* process was designed for professionals with professional expectations and considerations in mind. As such, many of the "what now, what next" questions can easily be anticipated and answered accordingly. Many already have been.

But not all. *Earning the Right to Be Heard* may be *good* science, but it's not *perfect* science. For example, do you really think it's possible for someone to *always* get what they want simply by applying the *Earning the Right to Be Heard* process? Of course not. Unfortunately, neither life nor this process works that way.

Sometimes the final response to our questions, inquiries, requests, and/or proposals must be "no." You don't have to like hearing "no," but you must learn to accept "no" in a professional manner when it comes—and it will.

Know this: if a decision-maker says "no" to your request, it doesn't necessarily mean he/she dislikes you or the initiative for which you are advocating. It's foolish and dangerous to assume such. The fact is, it's quite common for the decision-maker to like both you AND your initiative very much—but still reject the request.

Why? Actually, there are quite a number of possible reasons, including these most common ones: The timing of the request is not right. The current budget can't absorb the expenditure. The project payback doesn't meet pre-established standards. Other, more pressing organizational initiatives must take priority.

These reasons do not cast shade on your proposal. It's just business at work. The old saying "Sometimes you get the bear; sometimes the bear gets you" comes to mind. Sometimes you're successful in getting what you're hunting. Other times it seems like you become the hunted. Knowing both scenarios are possible should instill the necessary desire and willingness to do everything possible to get that bear (what you're hunting) first.

Wins and Losses

Here's a piece of unrequested advice for you to consider. Never fall into the habit of evaluating everything on the basis of aggregated wins and losses. Such a methodology may be good for determining conference and league sporting champions. But tallying wins and losses in life and work isn't nearly as clean or easy. In fact, some wins really don't matter much, whereas certain losses can yield great value.

For example, a young team member interviews for an internal promotion. It's a position she really wants. Unfortunately, the promotion goes to a more senior colleague. The young team member is disappointed. She feels the sting of the loss.

Yet during the process, the lead interviewer was favorably impressed with the rejected team member's preparation, communication skills, and determined effort. The interviewer recognized what she believed to be future potential based on how the young team member processed information and presented herself.

As a result, this previously "unsuccessful" candidate was ultimately invited to participate in a select management development program. The experience provided a heightened level of training and internal visibility for the

> **Some wins really don't matter much, whereas certain losses can yield great value.**

now better-prepared young woman. This combination of visibility and preparation led to a more significant position being offered and accepted, with even greater long-term opportunity on her professional horizon. Her initial "loss" (the first job opportunity) paled in comparison to the much more significant "win" (the second job opportunity). But the win wouldn't have been possible had it not been for the loss.

Or consider a second example. A customer becomes disgruntled regarding your perceived lack of responsiveness to his repeated service concerns. Seeing little evidence of change on your part, he becomes frustrated. His frustration eventually leads to shifting his business from you to your competitor. The economic loss is real.

Your surprise and embarrassment are real, too. You had been much too complacent. You realize that now. But rather than making excuses, you set about making amends. You begin by owning your mistakes and shortcomings. You undertake an overhaul of your service approach by identifying and correcting those failed policies, processes, and procedures that contributed to the earlier problems.

Once you're sure that your professional house is in order, you request a meeting with the former client. Putting your newly developed *Earning the Right to Be Heard* skill set to work, you describe and demonstrate a renewed level of awareness and professional commitment. Your primary objective is to win back the customer's trust. Your secondary objective is to regain his business.

Whether the customer actually returns or not, there has already been value in the experience. True transformation has taken place regarding your thoughts and actions. You've proven yourself to be better, sharper, and more intentional than before, even if that proof is recognized only by you. The original loss hurt. But the positive growth that resulted from the loss is an even bigger win.

"I Suck at Quitting"

I was contacted by a young engineer, then in his early-30s. He requested my professional help. After ten years with his firm, he was exploring a bold idea. Although he loved his job, his company, and his supervisor, he was considering a change. His daring plan involved voluntarily leaving his current employer in order to start his own independent engineering firm. He would not compete with his current employer for business. On the contrary, his plan involved moving to a smaller, more rural market, 250 miles away. His reasons for doing so? He desired an opportunity to build something on his own, he had discovered an area with untapped market potential, and he felt the area would improve the quality of life for his young family.

I listened carefully to his general plan. I was impressed. He knew what he wanted, and he was willing to do what he needed to realize his long-term objectives. His clear-eyed plan was rooted in desire, commitment, and optimism, yet grounded in realism regarding the necessary effort, sacrifice, and risk required. He also knew he needed a solid plan from which to work. That's where my input was requested.

"Phil, I know what I want to do. But I don't want to be rash or make foolish mistakes. I just need an honest, unbiased perspective to help me create and vet my working plan."

Unlike others employing the *Earning the Right to Be Heard* process, he was not building a plan to pitch to a decision-maker for approval. This was his personal decision to make and his alone. Still, I was sure the steps in the *Earning the Right to Be Heard* process could help in confirming or, possibly, redirecting his thinking.

During several conversations over several months, we revisited his idea. Together we explored the "five key questions" carefully: cost, benefit, time, implementation, and consequence. He took seriously the task of answering each question completely, in detail, along with the many related sub-questions uncovered along the way.

For the cost question, he developed a comprehensive working budget based on anticipated 18- to 24-month costs and conservative revenue estimates for a business start-up—the "new guy" in town. In considering benefits, among other things he created a detailed matrix of who his competition would be, evaluating their expertise, specialties, current client base, years before retirement, etc., then determining how his unique training and experience could differentiate him in his new marketplace.

And so it went, all five questions receiving careful consideration and planning. In time, the plan became more defined and detailed—a true working document. Eventually, his planning progress led to the inevitable questions, "What now and what next?"

"Phil, I've scheduled time with my boss next Tuesday," he reported to me one day. "I'm going to give my resignation notice then."

Up to this point, our exercise of developing and talking through "questions and answers," though serious, had been rooted in "what ifs." With his personal decision to move forward, he shifted definitively to "what now."

Nervous, but confident in his decision and preparation, he readied himself for the difficult resignation conversation. Remember, he wasn't running away from something he disliked. He was preparing to move to something he was convinced he would like better. He felt obligated to explain his decision in detail if his boss was interested. I requested a full report on the evening following the scheduled meeting. He agreed.

My phone rang. I had been anxiously awaiting this call. I couldn't help but wonder how things had gone. This was a huge decision and a big step to take. I got right to the point.

"So, how'd it go today?" I asked.

His response was unforgettable. The first words out of his mouth were these: "I suck at quitting."

His words were delivered with an almost embarrassed tone.

"You what?" I responded, genuinely confused.

"I suck at quitting," he repeated more emphatically.

I was still confused.

"So, you didn't resign after all?"

"No! I tried to, but he wouldn't let me! Apparently, I suck at quitting."

It was a funny line. It got better as the whole story unfolded.

Caught off guard by the unexpected resignation, the boss predictably began asking questions, as we've learned good decision-makers are inclined to do. The young engineer was ready with detailed answers. Although he didn't have written proofs specifically prepared, his knowledge and general preparations shone through. He walked his boss through his new business plan, including all the big questions—cost, benefit, time, implementation, and consequence. He provided detailed answers to his boss's additional questions with great clarity of thought and intention.

After the explanation had been completely offered came the ultimate surprise that neither he, nor I, nor virtually anyone could have imagined. Flatly refusing to accept the resignation, the boss, in turn, presented a counter-opportunity. He committed to setting the young professional up in his own engineering office. Specifically, it would be a new office, in the new market, with a new support staff, with a new title of general manager, all accompanied by a significantly increased compensation package.

In the span of one conversation, virtually all the risk, sacrifice, and uncertainty over which the young engineer had agonized for the past year was completely removed. He was being offered what he really wanted—expanded influence and new opportunities, in a new location and more.

Following a few days of thought and careful evaluation, the young engineer formally accepted the opportunity presented him. He continues to flourish in his new professional capacity.

"Man, he was lucky," some might say. I disagree. Luck had nothing to do with it.

During my high school football days, a saying was displayed prominently on the wall of our locker room. It read: "Luck is where preparation meets opportunity."

It's still true. The young engineer was not angling for a promotion or more money from his company. He just wanted autonomy, opportunity, and a new location. But because of his influence, preparation, and presentation he successfully secured all three—plus a promotion and enhanced compensation to boot.

The greatest advantage of all quite possibly is hiding in plain sight. That is, he's earned the right to be heard at all whole new level.

A Concise Review

The *Earning the Right to Be Heard* process is not intended to be a panacea—a one-size-fits-all solution for every difficulty. Each initiative envisioned is unique and should be approached that way.

The greatest advantage of all quite possibly is hiding in plain sight.

Although the initiatives might differ, the process should remain consistent.

A debriefing can be requested after any significant decision (positive or negative), but such meetings tend to be more helpful once you've learned you won't be getting what you had advocated for.

Here are four appropriate questions to ask during a post-decision debriefing:

- What did I do well?

- What could I have done better?

- What extenuating circumstances affected your decision that I could/should have recognized and controlled?

- What extenuating circumstances affected your decision that I would have had no control over?

Once decision-makers realize your capacity for understanding and applying rational problem-solving techniques to real-world organizational challenges, expect things to be forever changed.

Never fall into the habit of evaluating everything on the basis of aggregated wins and losses. In fact, some wins really don't matter much, whereas certain losses can yield great value.

CHAPTER 15

LOOSE ENDS

Transformation Begins Here

So what about you? You may not be a young engineer or a young anything. You may not be desirous of more autonomy, opportunity, or a location change. In fact, your career might actually be marked by more setbacks than comebacks. You're not asking for much. You just want to be taken seriously. You just want to *BE HEARD*. What are you going to do about that?

The course of a life and career is marked by a great number of transformational periods and experiences. Periodic transformations may take place when we leave home, start a job, retire, and so forth. Experiential transformation can happen when we get a promotion, fall in love, or even read a book. Possibly this book.

For some, just thinking about transformation can be an imposing, even daunting challenge. It shouldn't be. The process of transformation is truly no more than changing the structure, character, and/or appearance of something—or in this case someone. You.

In the past, whenever you've determined to change how you're doing something (structure), why you're doing something (character), and/or what it looks like (appearance), you've actually been on the cusp of personal transformation. Transformation of your choosing.

But being on the cusp (a point of transition between where you and where you wish to be) versus intentionally embracing a transformed reality are two very different states of being. Earlier in this book, planning and communicating were identified as being two essential steps in becoming a better leader and a more effective influencer. But as you recall, there was a third essential step. Execution. When all is said and done, it can't just all be said; it must be done.

The formula, template, process for selling ideas, building influence, and growing opportunities—it's all here in these pages. Once again, you're officially on the cusp. Now the time to execute, to get it done.

Charting Your Results

Since chapter 1, the importance of keeping priorities in proper order has been stressed. The "primary objective" has been, is, and will continue to be the same: a consistent effort to earn the right to be heard.

The "secondary objective" is just as firmly fixed. That is to get what we want and are truly willing to work toward. Keeping those priorities in order, one can expect to experience more significant wins than inconsequential losses. But allow those priorities to get scrambled, and the process inevitably heads in the wrong direction.

To keep these priorities straight, consider the four scenarios below. Then review the more in-depth description of each that follows.

CHARTING YOUR RESULTS[1]

WIN/WIN	LOSE/WIN
Congratulations, this is true cause for celebration.	Exceptionally short-term thinking.
You've accomplished BOTH objectives.	Yes, you got what you wanted— this time.
The opportunity for future influence is bright.	Don't expect it to happen repeatedly.

WIN/LOSE	LOSE/LOSE
A temporary, short-term disappointment.	This is absolutely the worst-case scenario.
Didn't get what you wanted— this time.	Future opportunities for influence are lost.
But the decision-maker listened to you.	Retraining and intentional trust-building is critical.

---

1   Thank you to Martin Ramsay (CEATH.com and LeadersOughtToKnow.com) for his role in helping shape the results matrix.

"LOSE/LOSE"

You **DID NOT** earn the right to be heard;
you **DID NOT** get what you wanted.

This is absolutely the worst-case *Earning the Right to Be Heard* scenario—your worst nightmare. There is no direction to go from here but up—unless, of course, you don't learn from your mistakes. Then you can expect to stay down. Like the other scenarios to be considered, this "LOSE/LOSE" outcome began with a desire to sell a decision-maker on a particular course of action—to influence his/her thinking. It fails dismally because no logical process is used to frame the initiative. With no logical process in place, no rational argument can be made to justify and support its approval. By using such a slipshod approach to influencing others, time is wasted (decision-makers are unhappy) and influence is squandered (idea sellers should be unhappy).

Considering this outcome, the idea seller ends up being worse off than if he/she had done nothing at all. The colossal failure creates an indelible black mark on the idea initiator's unwritten record. He/she had a legitimate opportunity but blew it. Decision-makers have long memories and are not apt to allow such a situation to recur, at least not one involving the same irresponsible idea initiator.

"LOSE/WIN"

You DID NOT earn the right to be heard, but you DID get what you wanted.

This is not the worst-case scenario (see the previous section). But please don't become satisfied simply because you got what you wanted. This position is uncomfortably close to being worst case and, therefore, should be plenty worrisome. Why? Because any cause for celebration in a "LOSE/WIN" outcome is bound to be short-lived and rarely repeated.

Various approaches can lead to this result. One such scenario is especially problematic. It catches decision-makers off guard, in their most vulnerable state. It's rife with situational emotion. If used by an idea seller to intentionally manipulate, the long-term results get uglier still. I won't describe it further here. I don't need to do so. I already have. If you need a reminder, just flip back to chapter 4, reread the section "Losing the Right to Be Heard," and you'll see why the "LOSE/WIN" scenario is so undesirable.

"WIN/LOSE"

You DID earn the right to be heard, but you DID NOT get what you wanted.

I get it. Not getting what you want is always disappointing, possibly discouraging. In the moment, hearing "no" is always tough to swallow. You legitimately worked hard to do everything right. With preparations made, you presented your case effectively, utilizing all the available *Earning the Right to Be Heard* bells and whistles. The process, intertwined with the wisdom of your years of work and related experiences, provided you with a formidable plan of attack. You were confident. Yet, no luck. You were admittedly unsuccessful at getting what it was you asked for and worked toward.

All that preparation and hard work. Was it worth it? you naturally wonder.

Of course it was! The *Earning the Right to Be Heard* process was created for situations like this and for dedicated people like you—situations in which you willingly take your best shot, never really knowing what the long-term results might be. Still, your dedication keeps moving you forward with a sense of expectancy.

As discussed earlier, many legitimate reasons exist for why a decision-maker might be compelled to reject even great ideas and pitches. They don't need to be rehashed again. What does need to be reemphasized is the frequently overlooked value of earning the ear (and trust) of decision-makers. Some discount the true value of access, trust, and influence entirely, because they're easy to overlook and difficult to measure. That's a seriously bad mistake. Remember, any time you genuinely and sincerely impress someone, that's a win. Every. Time. It's still a win, despite the fact that you may have lost the immediate opportunity to get what it was you wanted.

"WIN/WIN"

You **DID** earn the right to be heard;
you **DID** get what you wanted.

This scenario marks the pinnacle in advancing the broad scope of selling ideas, building influence, and growing opportunities. Accomplishments of this magnitude aren't given; they're earned. They don't happen often, or to everyone, or accidentally. Therefore, when they happen to you, that makes them all the sweeter. You're deserving. Congratulations! We won't dare take your accomplishment for granted. You're obviously doing several things right.

You've identified an issue of legitimate concern to others. You've suppressed those tempting, yet unproductive emotional responses and passionate arguments. Your focus is unwaveringly fixed on addressing issues from a logical perspective. You've examined available options in search of practical solutions. You've organized and presented those practical solutions alongside plausible benefits to be derived from them. You've communicated your support for the decision-maker's role. You've exhibited your desire to make a positive difference.

In this scenario, it's great to get what you want. Better still, you've impressed the decision-maker with your approach. Do good work and you can't be ignored. In fact, the decision-maker will want to hear more. That makes it official. You've proven yourself worthy of being heard.

What about Brenda?

One question still remains: *Of the four possible categories just outlined, which best describes where Brenda finished?*

We know for sure it wasn't "LOSE/LOSE" or "LOSE/WIN." How can we be sure? Simple. Brenda successfully made it through all "five key questions" (described in detail in chapters 8 through 13). Once asked, she successfully answered each question, providing suggested documentation (proofs) along the way.

Being able to move seamlessly through the five predictable questions provides the empirical evidence necessary to determine the decision-maker's interest and intention. With each question asked, the decision-maker revealed an interest in hearing/learning still more. Therefore, we can reasonably assume Brenda was successful in achieving no less than a legitimate "WIN/LOSE" position. Quite possibly, her efforts catapulted her into that hallowed "WIN/WIN" category.

Brenda's situation and success should not be considered unique or isolated. The success Brenda experienced is the same success available to every *Earning the Right to Be Heard* practitioner. From this day forward, the very LEAST that should be expected by those using the *Earning the Right to Be Heard* process is "WIN/LOSE" status. As the process is practiced and perfected, the number of "WIN/WIN" outcomes can be expected to increase as well. Along with both "WIN/LOSE" and "WIN/WIN" experiences come heightened levels of influence and opportunity.

The Process in Practice

The content contained in these pages is the direct by-product of hundreds upon hundreds of hours of personal development, professional application, and public examination. I developed a *technique for work*. I put that *technique to work*. Now I explain how the *technique can work* for others.

Over the past 25 years, professional and trade associations have adopted *Earning the Right to Be Heard* as a convention theme. Leadership conferences have featured the concept in keynotes and breakout sessions. Countless individuals have applied the principles of *Earning the*

Right to Be Heard to various projects and causes. Why? Because it's a value-added tool. It makes whatever you're selling—regardless of whether it's tangible or intangible; a product or an idea—more relevant.

Along the way, a great number of interesting interactions have occurred. Once, while sharing the proper steps for requesting an initial meeting with a decision-maker, a young workshop participant, apparently experiencing an epiphany, blurted out, "I didn't know a person was allowed to make recommendations to managers." I count that as a breakthrough.

Another time, months after participating in an *Earning the Right to Be Heard* session for young emerging community leaders, a 20-something put the technique to the test. She declared her candidacy for a seat on the local city council—and won—becoming the youngest city councilperson in that city's history. She later explained that *Earning the Right to Be Heard* was her catalyst—a clear-cut process by which she could sell her ideas directly to the voters.

But one doesn't need to be young, female, or an emerging politician to realize benefits from this technique. The opportunity is available to all.

Mere hours following the conclusion of a virtual *Earning the Right to Be Heard* training session, my phone rang. It was one of the online participants. The caller identified himself as a 35-year veteran of the construction industry, a trained professional engineer (P.E.) possessing extensive management experience.

He thanked me profusely for the practical methodology I had shared, adding that the session couldn't have come "at a better time." He explained how in three days' time, he would be making a huge presentation to his organization's board of directors. He would be presenting a capital request requiring an upfront $250,000 commitment. The request needed board approval.

Although the engineer had presented requests of varying sizes and complexities many times over the years, he admitted to being nervous. He explained how he had admittedly struggled, searching for the proper way to make such a "large ask," especially to a group of nontechnical (non-engineer) board members (decision-makers).

"As I was listening to you explain this concept, Phil, it clicked," he said. "It all made perfect sense. Your 'five questions' are key, but the proofs for each question make the real difference for me. I see that now. I think I can make the board see it, too."

He finished by sharing that he'd never been more excited about asking for a quarter of a million dollars, adding, "I just wish I had known about this technique 35 years ago. Who knows what difference that knowledge could have made in my career?"

FAQs

Like any other newly introduced technique, questions should be expected—and welcomed. Many important questions have already been posed and answered in preceding sections, but some questions don't fit neatly into the narrative of one chapter or another. They are unique enough to occupy their own category and require separate treatment. Here we call that category "FAQs" (Frequently Asked Questions). The following are a few random, yet frequently asked questions for your consideration.

FAQ #1:
Are some situations better suited to the
<u>Earning the Right to Be Heard</u> concept than others?

The *Earning the Right to Be Heard* process can be used effectively for almost any type of professional request. However, it seems to be most effective for unique, "one-off" type projects, initiatives, and/or undertakings.

In larger, more formally structured organizations, *Earning the Right to Be Heard* works well for "bigger" requests such as: capital projects, acquisitions, and/or market strategy initiatives. But for most readers, *Earning the Right to Be Heard* benefits will probably be best realized through "smaller" projects such as: process, procedural, and policy realignments and/or the requisition of business-specific support (i.e., manpower, machinery, and materials).

FAQ #2:
Is it detrimental that my boss (decision-maker) is familiar
with the <u>Earning the Right to Be Heard</u> process already?

Over the years, I've led dozens of *Earning the Right to Be Heard* workshops for corporate clients. Individual team members from manufacturing, mining, financial services, energy, utilities, agriculture, and health care organizations have been coached on how best to prepare for and respond to those "five key questions."

Often during a break in one of these workshops, a worried participant has pulled me aside to ask the following question: "Phil, I'm enjoying this workshop," he/she will begin, soft and low. "But did you know key decision-makers are in the room with us today? Is it good for them to know what you're teaching us?"

The question always makes me smile. Essentially, the participant is concerned that the decision-maker might balk if/when they realize the *Earning the Right to Be Heard* process is "being used on them."

"Don't worry," I always reassure them. "Your decision-makers know what I'm teaching. They hired me to share it with you. Learn the technique. Use the technique. It will make future decision-making more consistent for everyone—team members and decision-makers alike."

FAQ #3:
Who should be exposed to this technique?

This technique can have true and lasting value for almost any professional of any age and at any stage in their career. Individuals interested in selling more, influencing more, and/or growing (developing) more opportunities are wise to master this technique as early as possible.

Beyond the workplace, *Earning the Right to Be Heard* is especially worthwhile in classrooms as a practical offering to prepare vocational, college, and university students in their future career pursuits. Students preparing to begin their careers and enter the work world obviously should know what to expect. Of even more value is knowing in advance what decision-makers will expect of them.

FAQ #4:
Is this technique appropriate for use in general sales situations?

The *Earning the Right to Be Heard* technique is multifaceted. It can be used by almost anyone, in different situations, under varying conditions. The most common restriction to the use of this technique is not related to the technique itself but rather one's own imagination. If you can imagine how the technique might be used under differing circumstances, you should be able to find a way to make it work. One example is a common sales situation that many professionals encounter. For the sake of illustration, I'll use myself as the example.

For more than 30 years, I have owned and operated my own professional leadership development business. Many of my new business clients come as a result of referrals. It's not unusual for me to receive an unsolicited call that unfolds as follows:

(My office phone rings)

Me: *"Hello, Van Hooser Associates. This is Phil. How may I help you?"*

Caller: *"Are you the one who gives speeches and training sessions?"*

Me: *"Yes, that's what I do."*

Caller: *"How much do you charge?"*

(Pause)

Less than ten seconds into the call and I'm already presented with the most challenging question. Professionals responsible for selling almost anything generally agree that leading with the price is usually a sales no-no. Most find it far better to introduce available benefits before disclosing the price.

That is if *you* are leading the sales presentation. At this moment, I'm not. The prospect on the phone is in control of the dialogue. He/she called me. He/she asked me a direct question. As uncomfortable as I might be in the moment, to avoid or ignore the question altogether would almost certainly create some heightened level of frustration, tension, and possibly even animosity on the part of the caller. In such situations, I've found this to be a moment in which a stylized version of the *Earning the Right to Be Heard* approach can work in my favor.

(I respond)

Me: *"My fee is determined by program length, topic, and location. If you can give me a little more information, I'll be happy to quote you a price."*

(The caller is already exhibiting early, subtle signs of frustration)

Caller: *"Look, I need a speaker for a 90-minute presentation a week from Thursday in Atlanta. The topic is flexible. A colleague suggested you might be a good fit. So again, what do you charge?"*

(Pause)

To delay answering the question further is now riskier still. But so is *just* quoting a price. *Just* quoting a price often limits the opportunity for further discussion. In this case, it makes sense to reach into my *Earning the Right to Be Heard* bag of tricks.

(Resume)

Me: *"Thank you for sharing that information. I am available next Thursday. Therefore, my fee is $X,XXX."*

(Brief pause as caller mentally processes the fee. Does the caller feel the fee is too high? Too low? Unless they say directly, there's no way of knowing. There's really no time or reason to worry about that now. Instead, I unveil my "sales" version of *Earning the Right to Be Heard*.)

Me: *"Sir/Ma'am, I don't know if you've had the opportunity to check fees of other speakers, but if you have, you've probably discovered some are higher and some are lower than mine. The real determining factor, therefore, are the benefits you can expect from using my services."*

(I offer a pre-developed list of plausible benefits the client can expect.)

Me: *"But, as important as these benefits are, many of my clients are equally concerned about the timing of the presentation and how the presentation might be implemented to support the overall goals and objectives of the meeting you're planning."*

(I continue, going deeper, offering specific ideas about how the timing and implementation process might work best. Finally, I close with my consequences statement.)

Me: *"I realize there's a lot riding on the speaker you choose—possibly even the overall success of the entire meeting. Therefore, I'll remind you of the benefits you will realize should you choose to invite me to be your speaker in Atlanta."*

As with the traditional application approach of *Earning the Right to Be Heard*, one can never be absolutely sure of the decision that will ultimately be made. But this could conceivably be my only opportunity to communicate with this prospect. I at least want to have applied my best effort at both being hired and being heard.

By the way, for those who might be curious to know what happened with the prospect in question, consider this. My business was founded in 1988. I've been using some form of the *Earning the Right to Be Heard* sales process since at least 1993. I've been hired for over 4,500 live presentations. It's safe to say the process works more often than it doesn't.

Yesterday

It's been more than 20 years, but I remember the following experience as if it were yesterday.

I was contacted by the chief of police of a mid-sized police department. He asked if I was available to speak to his command staff during their upcoming annual training day. I was, and the date was set. When I asked about my topic, he displayed an unusual degree of indifference.

"Oh, it doesn't really matter," he said. "My staff hate these training days. But they must participate to get their credit hours for training required by state law. Frankly, I'll be satisfied if you just keep them awake for the three hours."

Although one of the more underwhelming professional challenges I'd ever received, nevertheless the chief's words inspired me. I set about developing a three-hour training session that would make a difference. I decided to include *Earning the Right to Be Heard* as its centerpiece.

The training day arrived, and the session was completed. The audience was far more engaged than the chief led me to expect, but the chief didn't know—he never showed.

On Friday of that same week, three days after the training session, I received an unexpected call. The caller identified himself as a lieutenant, a member of the chief's command staff. He had been in my earlier session.

"Phil, thank you for your presentation this week. Training sessions can be terribly boring and sometimes a waste. Not this one."

I was encouraged.

"Well, thanks for telling me so." Digging deeper, I asked, "Was there anything in particular that stood out to you from the training?"

"In fact, there was," he responded. "That's the reason I'm calling. The *Earning the Right to Be Heard* discussion really resonated with me." He continued, "Over the past several weeks, I had tried repeatedly to share a particular concern with our chief. I've had this idea for some time that I believe will improve the department's operations. But every time I've started to discuss it with the chief, he's interrupted me with one of his questions that he's so well known for. Nobody ever seems to be prepared for his questions, including me. Therefore, he just sends us away to research the answer. On those occasions when I've returned with an answer, I just get asked a different question.

"Honestly, I got fed up with it all. I decided to give up on sharing the idea with him entirely. It just wasn't worth it to me. That is, until your training session this week. As you talked, I began to realize the questions you were preparing us for were exactly the questions the chief had been asking me. Of course, I still didn't have the answers, so I decided to try it your way. Ever since our session, I've been busy researching and crafting answers and creating proofs as you suggested."

By now, I'm genuinely excited.

"That's wonderful!" I said, then asked with a chuckle, "So when are you going to meet with the chief to discuss these questions and your answers?"

"Yesterday," was his one-word reply.

He intentionally let the word linger before continuing.

"I had my meeting with the chief yesterday afternoon. We went through all his questions and my answers to those questions. It went great. In fact, he just now called and told me he would be approving the request that supported my idea. I thought you'd like to know."

"You were right! I love hearing success stories! Congratulations," I said. "I'm really happy for you."

"Thanks," he responded, "but there's one more thing. The chief told me that he didn't know where I learned to present ideas in such a formatted way but that he wished others knew how to do it, too."

We both laughed. Hopefully, the entire command staff now knew how to, as well.

Earning the Right to Be Heard as you sell ideas, build influence, and grow opportunities is always worth the effort. It's often fun, too.

A Concise Review

Keep your priorities straight: the "primary objective" is a consistent effort to earn the right to be heard, while the "secondary objective" is to get what we want and are truly willing to work toward.

From this day forward, the very LEAST that should be expected by those willing to sell ideas and build influence using the *Earning the Right to Be Heard* process is a "WIN/LOSE" outcome. As the process is practiced and perfected, the number of "WIN/WIN" outcomes can be expected to increase.

The *Earning the Right to Be Heard* process can be used effectively for almost any type of professional request and has true and lasting value for almost any professional of any age and at any stage in their career. Individuals interested in selling more, influencing more, and/or growing (developing) more opportunities are wise to master this technique as early as possible.

CONCLUSION

"It Doesn't Work!"

(My office phone rings)

Me: *"Hello."*

Caller: *"It doesn't work!"*

Me: *"I'm sorry, I'm confused. What doesn't work?"*

Caller: *"All that stuff you taught us about Earning the Right to Be Heard, that's what. It doesn't work."*

Me: *"Hold on, be more specific. What doesn't work?"*

Caller: *"I was in the Earning the Right to Be Heard workshop you led for our organization. Everything you talked about made sense. It made so much sense, I decided to try it for myself. I had an idea. So I decided to use your process to present my idea to the decision-maker in my organization. Just like you said."*

Me: *"Okay, go on."*

Caller: *"Well, I did everything you told us to do. I did my homework. I didn't rush in. I thought long and hard about my idea and the five questions to expect. I researched the costs and benefits. I developed a timeline and implementation plan. I created the proofs. I was ready. I requested a meeting with the decision-maker, just like you taught us."*

Me: *"Okay, everything was working for you up to this point, right?"*

Caller: *"Oh yeah, everything worked great—that is, right up until I got in the meeting."*

Me: *"So what happened then?"*

Caller: *"Well, I was a little nervous at first. But I delivered the opening statements I had prepared and rehearsed. I spoke up and said what I was there for and why I thought the timing was right to initiate my idea."*

(Long pause)

Me: *"And...?"*

Caller: *"And nothing! Nothing happened. That's why I called you. It doesn't work. Your process doesn't work. He didn't ask me any questions!"*

Me: *"No questions?"*

Caller: *"None! NOT ONE! When I finished my opening statement, he just said, 'Okay. Go ahead, show me what you've got.' Phil, you said he would ask the questions. He didn't. I froze. I didn't know what to do next."*

Me: *"Congratulations."*

Caller: *"Congratulations? What do you mean 'Congratulations'? For what?"*

Me: *"Congratulations on being in the best position possible—an even better position than I taught you. He didn't ask the questions. Instead, he left the door open for you to pose, then answer your own questions."*

Caller: *"What do you mean?"*

Me: *"When he said, 'Go ahead and show me what you've got,' you could have said, 'I have this idea, but I know it's your decision to make. So, I tried to put myself in your shoes. I imagined what questions you would need to have answered. Then I prepared answers to those key questions. Do you mind if share them with you now?' You had the opportunity to be in complete control of the conversation."*

(Long pause)

Caller: *"I guess that would've worked, too."*

Trust Yourself

"Life is the art of drawing sufficient conclusions from insufficient premises."

Those words are attributed to the English novelist Samuel Butler. But they seem equally appropriate as we conclude this comprehensive exploration of the *Earning the Right to Be Heard* process.

As you've carefully read and considered the information contained in these pages, you've certainly decided whether or not the process makes sense to you. You've arrived at your "sufficient conclusions."

But if you're the type who must have perfect conditions before taking action, well, good luck. Sufficient conclusions or not, perfect anything is a rarity. "Insufficient premises" are to be expected.

But for those individuals adventurous enough to move forward despite the imperfections around them, opportunity awaits. Those willing to take what they know and apply that knowledge to the many "insufficient premises" that exist are the ones who are equally bound to wring the most out of life, work, and the opportunities both provide.

Earning the Right to Be Heard is a critical tool to help you sell your ideas, build your influence, and grow your opportunities. But it requires you to translate understanding into action—to take initiative and take a chance. By giving your ideas life through this process, you will increase your self-confidence and satisfaction and expand your professional horizons. In fact, as you continually implement the *Earning the Right to Be Heard* system, be prepared to shift to the other side of it—eventually transitioning from idea initiator to decision-maker.

ABOUT THE AUTHOR

For 30-plus years, top US companies and organizations have trusted **Phillip Van Hooser, MBA, CSP, CPAE**, to show business professionals how to execute responsibilities while authentically connecting and engaging with people. As a result, thousands of people in hundreds of organizations have uncovered the real meaning of engaged leadership from the relatable, relevant illustrations and commonsense practices Phil uses. And in the process, they've discovered an arsenal of skills enabling them to achieve even greater personal and organizational results! A Hall of Fame keynote speaker, Phil is an expert on communication and leadership and the author of multiple business books, including *We Need to Talk: Building Trust When Communicating Gets Critical,* and *Willie's Way: Six Secrets for Wooing, Wowing, and Winning Customers and Their Loyalty.*

LET'S CONNECT!

Let's stay connected!

 https://www.linkedin.com/in/phillipvanhooser/

 https://www.youtube.com/user/philvanhooscr

 https://www.facebook.com/philvanhooser

 https://www.instagram.com/philvanhooser/

Or visit vanhooser.com for:

- Keynote presentations
- Leadership development training programs
- Executive coaching
- Online management courses
- More books, tools, and resources for success!

Van Hooser Associates, Inc.

vanhooser.com

hello@vanhooser.com

+1.270.365.1536

MORE TITLES TO SUPPORT YOUR SUCCESS

Leaders Ought to Know:
11 Ground Rules for Common Sense Leadership

We Need to Talk:
Building Trust When Communicating Gets Critical

Willie's Way:
Six Secrets for Wooing, Wowing, and Winning Customers and Their Loyalty